ALLIGATORS & CROCODILES

ALLIGATORS & CROCODILES

Malcolm Penny

CRESCENT BOOKS
NEW YORK

This 1991 edition published by Crescent Books, distributed by Outlet Book Company, Inc., a Random House Company, 225 Park Avenue South, New York, New York 10003.

Color reproduction in Hong Kong by Fotographics
Typeset by M.C. Typeset Limited, Gillingham, Kent
Printed and bound in Hong Kong

ISBN 0-517-07012-X

87654321

Designed and edited by
Anness Publishing

ACKNOWLEDGEMENTS

All pictures courtesy of Ardea London Ltd.: Jack Bailey 40; Ian Beames 56, 59, 65, 78 top, 106; Hans & Judy Beste 19; Donald D. Burgess 100; M.D. England 60, 61 top; Jean-Paul Ferrero 14, 85, 86, 94, 95, 97, 107, 121 top; Kennith W. Fink 25, 51, 101, 114, 117; Bob Gibbons 89 top; Francois Gohier 70, 99, 103, 112 top; Nick Gordon 8, 46, 47, 71, 76, 108, 119; Martin W. Grosnick 35, 49, 126; Joanna van Gruisen 28, 44 below; 45, 54, 74, 75, 80–84; Masahiro Iijima 73, 98; M. Krishnan 66; J.M. Labat 67 below; Keith & Liz Laidler 87, 118; E. Lindgren 48, 123; John Mason 55, 67 top, 68, 69, 122, 124; Pat Morris 44 top, 89 below, 110 top, 125, 127; D. Parer & E. Parer-Cook 121 below; Tomistoma Schlegeli 88; Peter Steyn 52, 53; John E. Swedberg 50, 102, 116; Ron & Valerie Taylor 96; Balaram Thapa 115; McDougal Tiger-Tops 104, 105, 112 below; Richard Waller 78 below; Adrian Warren 42, 43, 58, 61 below, 62, 63, 64 top, 72, 90, 92, 93, 110 below, 111, 113, 120; C. Weaver 64 below; Alan Weaving 79; Wardene Weisser 11.

CONTENTS

FOREWORD

One dewy early morning in Chitwan National Park, in Nepal, I was riding an elephant, looking for one-horned rhinos. We came to the Rapti River, wide and shallow at that point, and made to cross. The elephant stopped at the bank, trembling, and would go no further. When the mahout clouted it on the head with his iron goad, it tensed its whole body and trumpeted shrilly through its raised trunk. The mahout said one of the few words of Nepali I could understand: 'Mugger'. The Indian marsh crocodile.

Although the danger is minimal, elephants are terrified of muggers. Our elephant would not go into the water until the dark shape had glided away along the bank, driven by a couple of clods of earth flung by the mahout. We humans are not alone in our fear of crocodiles.

Later that same year, in Florida, I stood among a dozen sightseers in the Everglades, gazing from a boardwalk at a group of somnolent alligators. One of them slid into the water and disappeared without a ripple. We leaned forward to see better, fascinated from behind the safety of the rail.

This combination of fear and fascination is what draws people to contemplate the crocodilians. The reward for a closer look at this ancient group of reptiles is a glimpse into a prehistoric world.

Malcolm Penny

INTRODUCTION

If crocodilians had not survived into the modern world, their fossilized remains would have been as much of a puzzle as those of their close relations, the dinosaurs. But they did survive, giving us an insight into an animal way of life many millions of years old, and still successful in a world dominated by mammals.

Their success arises partly from their giant size: they are archosaurs, the last of the 'ruling reptiles'. They are fearsome to behold, including among their number some of the few animals which regularly regard humans as prey. Myths and legends have grown up around them, and they have been persecuted – or worshipped – for many centuries. Modern biology has discovered aspects of their life which would have been unthinkable to the ancients: they can be gentle, even sensuous, towards their mates and their young.

The evolution of crocodilians as well as the behaviour patterns and differences between the various species are examined in this section providing a thorough introduction into the complex and misunderstood world of alligators and crocodiles.

CROCODILIANS
Of Giants and Dragons

The crocodilians are members of an order of reptiles consisting of the alligators, the gharial, and the true crocodiles. They are the last survivors of the great group of 'ruling reptiles', the archosaurs. Among their extinct relatives, the best-known are the mighty dinosaurs. All descended from common ancestors, the thecodonts, which flourished during the early Triassic period, 225 million years ago. The fossil record shows that modern crocodilians have changed very little since they first appeared, about 160 million years ago, in the midst of an unexplained increase in the numbers of huge reptiles. When that surge died down about sixty-five million years ago, at the end of the Cretaceous period, and the rest of the archosaurs disappeared – an equally unexplained event – most of the crocodilians survived. They are the largest living reptiles in the world, fearsome and widely feared.

COLD-BLOODED HORROR

There is something about the combination of great size and cold blood that inspires horror in humans. Elephants or gorillas are larger, but they are mammals like ourselves, intelligent, with a family life. Even lions and tigers are less awesome: after persecution by generations of hunters, all but the sick or deranged steer well clear of mankind. We credit whales with great intelligence, and there are many stories of their gentle behaviour. But crocodilians have no fear, and except in their parental behaviour they are by no means gentle. They are predators, of relatively limited intelligence, and when they see a meal, they take it, whether it has four legs or two. The dread in which they are held by most of the human race has hastened several species towards extinction. Fear has unleashed many a spear, and driven many a bullet to its mark.

ANCIENT OR MODERN?

They may be ancient, but crocodilians are not primitive in reptilian terms. Their breathing apparatus is highly developed and specialized. The nostrils are placed at the very tip of the snout, so that the animal can breathe when the rest of its body is submerged; a vital aid to camouflage when it is hunting. A secondary palate and a flap at the base of the tongue enable crocodilians to close off the windpipe, and thus to open the mouth under water when they seize their prey. They have a partition separating the chest from the rest of the body cavity, rather like the diaphragm of mammals. This partition can be moved by means of a muscle, so that crocodilians can breathe more efficiently than other reptiles.

The crocodilian heart, too, is closer to that of a mammal than to those of other reptiles, giving them a more efficient circulatory system. In most reptiles the heart has three chambers. Oxygenated blood from the lungs and oxygen-exhausted blood from the muscles and internal organs arrives in separate auricles, but is then mixed in a common ventricle. The result is that some of the blood being pumped out into the general circulation is oxygen-deficient, not having passed through the lungs to be recharged. In the heart of a crocodilian, the ventricle is divided into two parts by a partition, so that de-oxygenated blood goes only to the lungs and only freshly oxygenated blood passes into the circulation.

These features make crocodilians especially interesting to biologists. As the only living relatives of the great dinosaurs, they provide a clue to the adaptations which may have made the dinosaurs so successful for such a long period in the animal history of the earth.

DRAGONS FROM FAR AWAY

When the first explorers returned from Egypt to Greece and Rome, they brought back stories of these powerful predators. Although their reports were factual, they must have been hard to believe, and legends inevitably grew up around them. It cannot have been long before these stories stirred recollections of ancient accounts of other great reptiles, sprung not from travellers' tales but from the imagination of story-tellers, or even from some distant folk-memory of days when crocodilians still flourished in Europe and North America – and dragons were thus reborn.

Long before the Greeks and Romans, the Egyptians had first-hand knowledge of crocodiles, from the cradle of their civilisation along the banks of the Nile. They regarded them with awe, and soon included a crocodile, Sebek, among their gods. Its embodiment on earth was a series of sacred

The cold, hooded gaze of an American alligator. Of limited intelligence compared with mammals, crocodilians are perceived as fearless hunting machines of great size and strength. As such, they inspire terror and the urge for vengeance in humans.

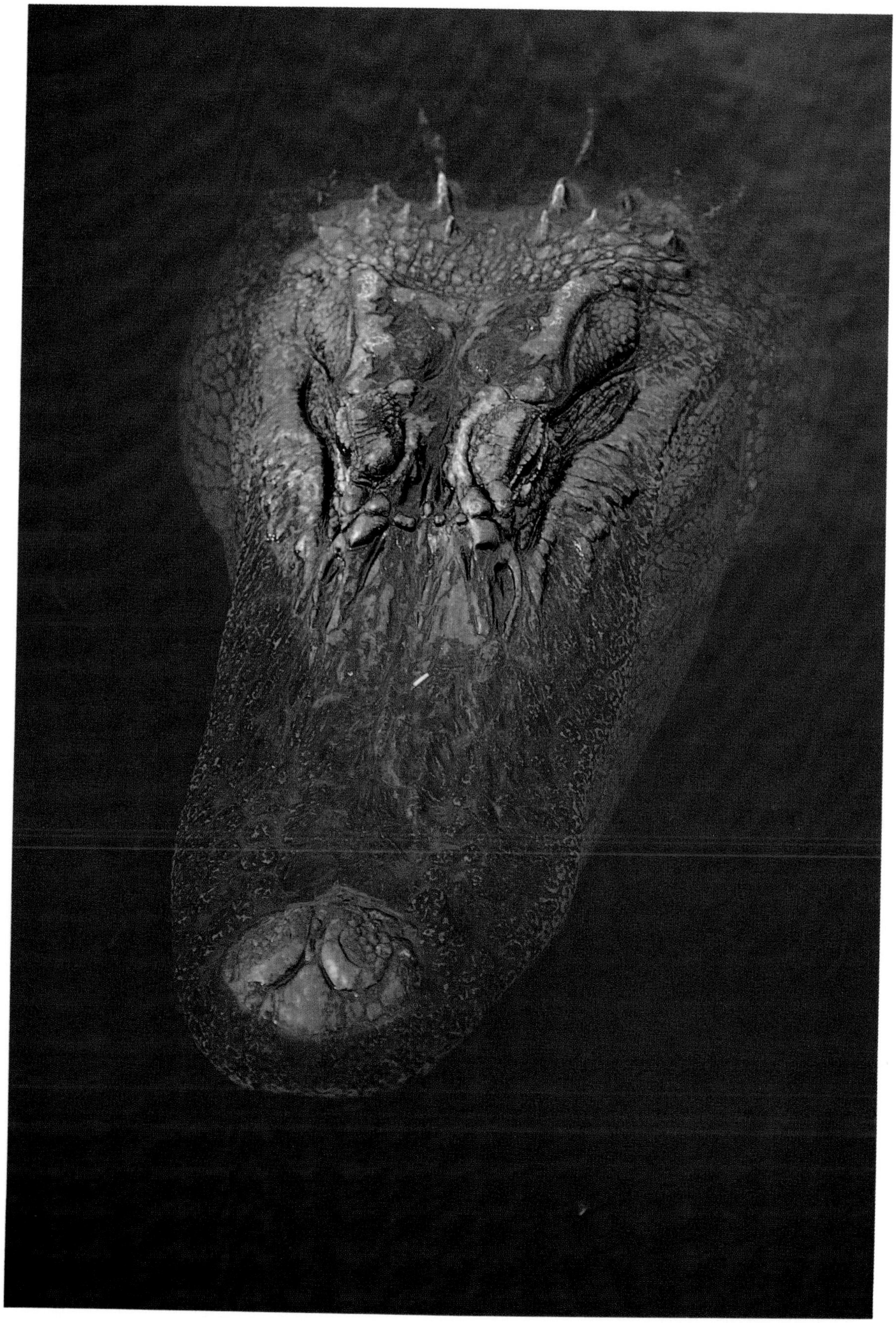

crocodiles, which were pampered by priests, being given cakes and wine. These crocodiles were embalmed when they died, and buried in sacred cemeteries. Herodotus, in about 450 BC, and Strabo (63 BC – AD 20) both visited and wrote about the sacred crocodiles.

Such were the accounts that came down to the medieval bestiarists, who were not myth-makers but serious scholars, albeit working entirely from texts. They described dragons as great reptiles, often attributing to them enormous cunning and strength, enough to outwit and kill elephants. Dragons were generally said to live 'in Ethiopia and India, in places where there is perpetual heat'. Indeed, maps of these countries were often labelled with the heart-stirring inscription 'Here Be Dragons'.

The same bestiarists knew of crocodiles from their classical studies. (The Romans had collected crocodiles for their spectacular circuses, usually from the lower reaches of the Nile.) One such scholar described a crocodile, in a memorable phrase, as 'armed with an awfulness of teeth and claws'; he knew that crocodiles hatch their eggs in sand, that they are amphibious, and that they have armoured backs. However, because zoology was in those days an armchair pastime, based on the writings of previous authors, and on examination of the relics brought back, often long before, by travellers in distant lands, the dragon and the crocodile survived side by side for centuries. More recent studies have replaced the dragon where it belongs, in the realm of fantasy – or folk-memory – and installed the crocodile in its proper place in the animal kingdom, as the last living relative of the dinosaurs.

CROCODILIAN EVOLUTION
The Fossil Record

The palaeontologist Rodney Steel wrote of crocodilians in 1989: 'Had they failed to survive into the modern world, their petrified bones would have been just as much a source of wonder and speculation as the skeletons of their close relatives, the dinosaurs'. In fact, the fossil record of crocodilians is very long and complete, and, as he implied, the remains are easier to interpret than those of other archosaurs because we have a variety of living species with which to compare them.

The earliest crocodilians, those which flourished alongside the dinosaurs, were somewhat more primitive than those of today. Although there were crocodilians of the modern type alive at the time, they were in a minority. The dominant group is known as mesosuchian ('middle crocodilian'), as compared with the modern type, which is called eusuchian ('true crocodilian').

The differences between them are subtle, but they clearly distinguish the older design, which was successful for so long, from the newcomers, whose time was yet to come. Mesosuchians had a secondary palate whose hinder part was made of cartilage rather than bone, and a spine whose articulation was weaker than that of modern crocodiles. Some had primitive features in the skull, such as a protuberant bar behind the eye; others lacked the bony eustachian tube connecting the ear and the throat, which is common to all modern crocodilians.

However, they all shared one feature which links them to the distant common ancestors of all crocodilians, dinosaurs, and birds — the thecodonts: this is the way in which the feet are joined on to the legs.

THE THECODONT ANKLE

In most reptiles the two upper ankle bones, the calcaneum and the astragalus, move with the long bones above them, the tibia and fibula. In crocodilians — and in thecodonts — the joint passes between the two upper bones, so that the calcaneum is part of the foot. A peg on the astragalus fits into a socket in the calcaneum, producing a joint which can withstand the strong twisting movements used during the 'high walk' (see 'Locomotion', page 15). It may have been this apparently trivial difference from other reptiles which gave the mesosuchians the advantage which enabled them to dominate the crocodilian scene until they were gradually overtaken by the more efficient eusuchians about sixty million years ago.

In the late Triassic period, some crocodilians were fast-moving land predators. One such was *Terrestrisuchus*, found in the Upper Triassic in England. It had long, slender limbs with short claws, adapted for running. This suggests that it caught its prey in its jaws. Another was *Ticinosuchus*, which grew over 6m (20 ft) long. The Triassic crocodilian *Desmatosuchus*, from what is now the southern

United States, was shaped much more like a modern crocodilian, but its simple teeth suggest that it fed mainly on plants.

A BLIND ALLEY, AND A GIANT

Alongside the crocodilians that are plainly related to modern species lived other descendants of the thecodonts called phytosaurs. Although they looked superficially like modern fish-eating crocodiles such as the gharial, phytosaurs had their nostrils far back on their snouts, indicating that they were not as well-adapted to an amphibious life.

The largest fossil crocodilian known is called *Deinosuchus*, the 'terror crocodile'. It is found in the late Cretaceous period in North America, in locations as widely separated as Montana, Texas, Delaware, and Georgia, in fossil-beds which were laid down seventy million years ago. Its lower jaw is 2m (7ft) long, and its overall length must have been in the region of 15m (50ft). Its weight has been estimated at over six tonnes. Its bones are always found in association with the remains of dinosaurs, especially the plant-eating duck-billed dinosaurs, also known as hadrosaurs. Until these gigantic bones were discovered it had been thought that the chief predators on hadrosaurs were tyrannosaurs — the largest land-based carnivores ever to have lived. Now it seems as though they were the prey of crocodiles besides which today's saltwater crocodiles — the largest modern terrestrial carnivores — look like juveniles.

A CHANGE OF CLIMATE

The end of the Cretaceous period, about sixty-five million years ago, is notable for the sudden wave of extinction which swept the world. The dinosaurs disappeared in a moment of geological time — it may have been several million years, though some scientists have suggested that it was little more than a century. The cause of this catastrophe is not known, but theories to account for it are often based on the idea of a cataclysmic event, such as the impact of a giant meteor. Clouds of dust cover the earth, in some versions, blotting out the sun for years, and causing the death of most plant life and all the large animals dependent on plants. The definition of 'large' is usually 'over 34kg'. When the dust clears, the dinosaurs are dead.

There is evidence that something of the kind happened. A very thin layer of rare metals such as iridium and osmium can be found exactly at the dividing line between the Cretaceous and Palaeocene periods, and proponents of the theory say that the metals must have come from a meteorite or comet. Whatever the cause, the Cretaceous extinction happened: but it did not happen to all large reptiles. As we know, the crocodilians survived.

THE SURVIVAL OF THE CROCODILIANS

There are theories to explain how they did it. The most attractive is that whatever climatic event hit the rest of the world's population had least impact on freshwater communities, of which the crocodilians were a part. They depended neither on marine plankton nor on flowering plants, both of which were severely disrupted at the time, and were therefore able to sustain themselves by other means.

They went on surviving through most of the Tertiary era. Until thirty-five million years ago they flourished in North America and Europe alongside plants whose living relatives are now found only in tropical or subtropical environments. At the time when those plants disappear from the fossil record in northerly latitudes,so do the crocodilians. That date is usually placed somewhere before the start of the Pleistocene Ice Age, about two million years ago. At that time there was a substantial drop in mean annual temperatures in the world as a whole, resulting in huge changes in local floras — and the redistribution of the crocodilians.

The distribution of crocodilians today may therefore reflect the climate of North America and Europe two million years ago. Crocodiles do not live where the temperature regularly falls below 10°–15°C (50°–59°F): they are thus restricted to the tropics and subtropics. American alligators can survive much lower temperatures, down to 4°C (39°F), and remain active at temperatures of 12°–15°C (54°–59°F), though their optimum is 32°–35°C (90°–95°F). Their distribution reflects this wider tolerance of low temperatures.

THE LIFE OF GIANT REPTILES

TEMPERATURE CONTROL

Being reptiles, crocodilians are poikilothermic, a condition usually — and misleadingly — called 'cold-blooded'. The word really means that they tend to take on the temperature

The Australian saltwater crocodile is the largest of all crocodilian species, capable of growing to a length of 9m (30ft). Larger specimens have been reported, the longest being a sacred crocodile in North Borneo, whose impression on a sandbank was measured at 10m (33ft).

of their surroundings, having no internal control of their own temperature. Although they can tolerate a fairly wide range of temperatures, from about 5°C (41°F) to 38°C (101°F), they function most efficiently between 30°–35°C (90°–95°F). There is some evidence that certain large species are able to control their internal temperature independently of their surroundings, but, as we have seen, poikilothermy is the main factor limiting the distribution of crocodilians through the world.

Large size is an advantage to such animals, since their surface area is relatively small compared to their volume. This means that they lose or gain heat more slowly than they would if they were smaller. Nevertheless, crocodilians have to find ways of maintaining their temperature near the optimum even in their home in the tropics, where the temperature changes between day and night may be really quite marked.

Living near water enables them to counter these changes by quite simple tactics. Water is slow to lose or gain heat, and the crocodilians can use it as a buffer between themselves and the temperature of their environment. When the sun rises, the animals emerge from the water where they have spent the night — water which has probably cooled considerably since the previous evening — to bask in the sun for a time. Having warmed up, they slip back into the water when the sun becomes too hot. Such movement to and from the water to maintain a relatively consistent temperature shapes the pattern of a crocodilian's day.

Crocodilians are often seen lying on the bank of a pool or stream with their mouths wide open. This has been said to be a means of lowering their temperature (by allowing moisture to evaporate from the lining of the mouth), or in some cases raising it (by exposing the highly vascular lining of the mouth to the sun). However, since it is seen even in the cool of early morning, it may have another function, either as a threat in response to some distant alarm, or even as a way of drying out the lining of the mouth to reduce the chance of infestation by algae or fungi.

Seasonally, the animals may have to compensate for more drastic changes. Where there is a prolonged dry season or a markedly cooler winter period, they often become torpid, feeding only occasionally, and retreating to some quiet corner until better conditions return. This is not hibernation in the true sense, but more a means of husbanding their resources by adopting a lower metabolic rate.

LOCOMOTION

On land, crocodilians may give the impression that they are sluggish creatures, crawling slowly on their bellies, or stirred into sudden movement only by some alarm, whereupon they slither rapidly into the water. Most species can walk perfectly well, however, being able to raise their bodies off the ground and then striding along rather like a mammal. Such a gait is sometimes called a 'high walk', to distinguish it from the more usual leisurely crawl. The Indian marsh crocodile or mugger often travels long distances over land in a high walk.

There are exceptions. Although they can move swiftly and with great power when swimming, the gharial and the saltwater crocodile have weak legs, and seldom move more than a few metres from water. The Australian freshwater crocodile, in contrast, can gallop like a squirrel across dry ground even when it is fully grown, a gait which is used by other crocodilians only when they are very small.

In water, crocodilians swim strongly and well, using the tail alone, the efficiency of which is improved by the vertical ridge of scales that increases its area. The limbs are carried tucked against the body. Even though the back feet are webbed, they are not used in swimming: the webbing is an emergency escape mechanism. In sudden panic, a crocodilian will move its hind feet sharply upwards with the webbing spread. This causes it to crash dive backwards beneath the surface.

FEEDING AND DIGESTION

Crocodilians are carnivorous — scavengers as well as predators. They will eat anything they can kill, including other crocodilians. As an individual grows larger, its range of prey increases to include larger animals.

Hunting is usually carried out by stealth and sudden movement, whether a small alligator is catching a water bug, or a large one a heron. Nile crocodiles lurk beneath the surface close to the edge of pools where animals come to drink, seizing their prey by the snout and dragging it into the water to drown. Indian marsh crocodiles have been seen to kill cattle in this way, and Australian saltwater crocodiles occasionally attack human beings, leaping suddenly out of the water after approaching submerged from a position several metres away.

Digestion is slow, in keeping with the low metabolic rate of reptiles. When food is plentiful and it is able to gorge itself, a large crocodilian needs to eat only about once a week. The meal might take it four to five days to digest, depending on the temperature. In cool weather, below 20°C (68°F), some of the crocodilians in one experiment refused to feed at all, presumably because their digestive systems had stopped working.

STONES IN THE STOMACH

Much has been written about gastroliths, which are stones or other hard objects found in the stomachs of all crocodilians over one year of age. Their importance to the animals is shown by the fact that even crocodilians living in muddy places where stones are hard to find always have their complement of gastroliths: in some cases the pebbles involved have been shown to come from several miles away. In a reflection of our modern age, gastroliths collected recently from crocodilian stomachs have included bottles, cartridge cases, a Thermos flask, coins, and pieces of plastic.

Once it was thought that they were used as ballast, to help the animal to dive or to give it greater stability in the water; but it has been pointed out that gastroliths make up only about one per cent of an animal's weight, so that they would be unlikely to have much effect. A more likely reason for their presence is to aid digestion: in fact, an experiment with X-rays showed that a caiman's stomach became suddenly active 36 hours after it had been fed with a dead mouse, the gastroliths churning around 'like pebbles in a cement mixer' until the mouse was unrecognizable. The use of gastroliths to aid digestion in birds is well known, and it also seems the most plausible reason for their presence in crocodilians.

REPRODUCTION

The courtship of crocodilians may be a noisy business. Male alligators roar loudly as they lie in the water, their whole bodies vibrating so that rows of little fountains leap from the water where it covers their backs. Others nearby join in, making the mating season a dramatic chorus of alarming bellows. Male Nile crocodiles cough or bark, occasionally making a deep rumbling noise with their mouths wide open.

Rival males fight fiercely amongst themselves, either to defend a site on the shore, or to drive another male away from a nearby female. Loss of limbs is common in these fights, and one male not infrequently kills the other.

Once a male has attracted and been selected by a female, things become quieter, as the pair swim slowly side by side until she permits him to mate. Nile crocodiles have a particularly gentle courtship ritual. After the female has demonstrated her submission, with a distinctive arching movement in which her head and tail are briefly submerged, the male responds by rubbing his head to and fro across the female's neck as a prelude to mounting her. American alligators perform similar movements: it has been said that they produce a scent from glands in the throat at the time, and that the scent stimulates the female.

EGG-LAYING AND NESTING

Being reptiles, crocodilians lay eggs with hard shells, which most species bury in holes dug in a shady place near water. The male usually plays no further part in the process — he probably mated with several females during the season — but the female guards the nest site for ten or twelve weeks until the eggs hatch. The most common egg-predators on crocodilian nests in Africa are monitor lizards and wild dogs; in America, raccoons take alligator eggs if the female leaves the nest unattended for too long. When the eggs hatch, the babies make croaking noises which the mother can hear. A female Nile crocodile loosens the soil above them at this time by wriggling on it and digging to break up the ground surface. She then escorts or carries the newborn crocodiles to the water.

American alligators, Australian saltwater crocodiles, and some caimans make a nest on the surface of the ground, by piling vegetation into a circular heap, and laying their eggs within it. The vegetation produces heat as it rots, incubating the eggs at a constant temperature of 30°–32°C (86°–90°F) while the mother guards the nest. While she waits, the mother American alligator digs out a pool near the nest, which she will use as a nursery for the youngsters.

Babies in these piled up 'compost nests' do not attempt to leave the mound when they hatch. They remain in the eggshell with only their snouts protruding, and squeak when they feel the vibrations caused by their mother moving nearby. In response, she opens the nest-mound and carries the babies away, often cracking with her jaws any eggs which have not hatched, to liberate the baby inside. The American alligator female carries her young to the nursery pool which she has been digging nearby while they were in their eggs.

There are intriguing variations in this pattern among the crocodilians of the world, as will become apparent in the following section on individual species.

GROWING UP AS A CROCODILIAN

The female American alligator has been known to care for her young for as long as four years after they have hatched, but this is probably an exceptional period for crocodilians as a whole. The broad-nosed caiman, in eastern South America, protects its young for a year, with both parents sharing the duty. Small saltwater crocodiles are protected by their mother for about ten weeks before they depart to make their own way in the world, while in Nile crocodiles maternal care is thought not to extend beyond the first few weeks of life.

When the wet season arrives young crocodilians may move off in a group into secluded shallow backwaters, where food is abundant but larger animals are scarce, so that they can concentrate on learning to fend for themselves. The young of some species are frequently found in damp vegetation some distance from water, safe from the attentions of larger crocodilians which would regard them as food.

All small crocodilians suffer heavy losses from a variety of predators, from storks, eagles, and herons to mammalian predators, turtles, and even large fish. Many are able to summon parental assistance in times of emergency by uttering distress calls, usually in the form of high-pitched squeaks which carry a long distance across water.

Depending on the species, crocodilians reach sexual maturity at between four and ten years of age. Until they are fully grown, they tend to congregate in groups of roughly the same size, to minimize the danger of being attacked and maimed or killed by larger animals. In some species there are appeasement rituals which indicate submission and tend to disarm an aggressive senior male, but evidently these are not to be relied on; most species are cannibalistic.

LIVING CROCODILIANS OF THE WORLD

Like crocodiles round a drowned buffalo, the taxonomists tussle over the family Crocodylidae, debating whether it is divided into three or four parts, or subfamilies. The argument is all but hypothetical, since the subfamilies in question are tiny. Although the dwarf crocodile has some characteristics in common with the caimans, which are alligators, it is usually listed with the true crocodiles; and the false gavial (or gharial — the reader will encounter both transliterations from the Hindi name) may or may not be in a subfamily of its own, and not a crocodile after all. For the purposes of this list, both will be put at the end of their respective families, whence they may be repositioned to taste.

The visible distinction between the two large subfamilies, crocodiles and alligators, is in the arrangement of their teeth; specifically the large fourth tooth in the lower jaw. In alligators, it is invisible when the mouth is closed, since it fits into a socket in the upper jaw: in crocodiles, it can be seen, where the upper jaw is notched to make room for it. There is no other visible difference between the subfamilies, though clear differences in the structure of the skull and the ventral scales are enough to distinguish them for taxonomic purposes. This distinction is justified by differences in the typical behaviour and distribution of the two reptilian groups.

CROCODILES: Subfamily Crocodylinae

NILE CROCODILE

Crocodylus niloticus

DISTRIBUTION: Throughout tropical and subtropical Africa, and Madagascar, except the Kalahari and Sahara deserts. Nile crocodiles lived in the Seychelles until 1819, and they are occasionally reported from the Comoros. There were isolated populations in the Saharan mountains and in Mauritania until the 1930s. Their numbers are much reduced in most parts of this range now, because of overhunting.

HABITAT: A wide range of freshwater habitas, but also coastal areas in West Africa. They are occasionally washed out of river mouths into the sea: one was reported 11km (7 miles) off the coast of Zululand, and the species frequently reaches Zanzibar off the East African coast.

APPEARANCE AND SIZE: Adults are dark olive green, paler beneath; the crossbands on the tail tend to become less obvious with age. Juveniles are greenish on the back, with darker, irregular crossbands, especially on the tail. Adults grow to a maximum of 6m (20ft); records of shot specimens include 6.5m (21ft 4in) (Tanzania 1905), 6.4m (21ft) (Uganda 1948), 5.94m (19ft 6in) (Uganda 1953), and 5.87m (19ft 3in) (Botswana 1968). The pressure of hunting is such that few have the chance to grow to their maximum potential. A population in the Aswa River in northern Uganda is said to reach a maximum length of only 2m (7ft), with disproportionately large heads: this is thought to be because they live in a difficult environment, with a long dry season during which they cannot feed, so that their normal annual growth is restricted.

REPRODUCTION: Females are sexually mature at ten years (when they are about 2m/7ft). They lay their eggs in holes, the clutch size (number of eggs) averaging fifty, with a maximum of eighty. Incubation takes eleven to thirteen weeks, but may be longer in cooler climates. Mothers assist the young in emerging from the egg, and protect them for some weeks after hatching.

DIET: The diet of most crocodilians varies with age. Nile juveniles take insects and frogs, snakes and other small vertebrates, graduating to fish as they grow. Large adults can take antelope, including wildebeeste, zebra, domestic stock, and humans.

SALTWATER CROCODILE

Crocodylus porosus

DISTRIBUTION: This is the most widely distributed of all crocodilians. It occurs throughout the tropical regions of Asia and the Pacific, from the west coast of India, through Sri Lanka, Bangladesh, the Malay Peninsula, Indonesia and the Philippines, New Guinea, and northern Australia, to the Solomon Islands and Fiji. (There are even records from Burma and southern China.) 'Salties' are often seen far out to sea: the species has reached the Cocos Islands 1000km (625 miles) from the nearest land.

HABITAT: In spite of its name, the species is not exclusively marine or estuarine. It is often found in lakes or large rivers, as far as 1130km (706 miles) inland in New Guinea.

APPEARANCE AND SIZE: Adults range from grey through tan to dark olive, often with large black spots on the back and sides, but paler beneath. The extent of the dark coloration may be determined by the colour of the natural background in which they grew up. The scales on the back are regular, and noticeably oval in shape. Juveniles are more brightly coloured, with spots and blotches on the tail which often coalesce to form bands. This is the largest of all extant crocodiles, growing to 9m (30ft) if it is allowed to live long enough. The largest specimen in modern times may have been a sacred crocodile in North Borneo, whose impression in a sandbank measured 10m (33ft). A reasonably reliable record of a shot specimen measured 8.64m (28ft 4in) (Australia 1957); other reports have usually turned out to be exaggerated when the crocodile is measured accurately after the excitement of the hunt has cooled.

REPRODUCTION: Saltwater crocodiles are sexually mature at ten to fifteen years, which normally means a length of 2m (7ft) for females and 3m (10ft) for males. Eggs are laid during the wet season in a mound nest; the clutch size is anything from twenty to ninety. Incubation is usually thirteen weeks. Maternal care has often been reported, the female shepherding and guarding the young for up to two-and-a-half months.

DIET: Juveniles eat insects, crabs, lizards and snakes. Large adults will take any mammal near to water, including sambhar, cheetah, monkeys and wild pig. In northern Australia, feral buffalo and large kangaroos form part of the diet. Large domestic animals are often taken, and there are many records of predation on humans. Salties kept in captivity for study have been known to stalk their keepers, and attack them if they venture too close to the edge of the pool in which the crocodiles are kept. Fish, including sharks, and marine turtles, cormorants and geese have been found in saltwater crocodile stomachs.

OPPOSITE PAGE

The back of a saltwater crocodile is protected by long oval scutes, but its dermal armour is less massive than that of other crocodiles. This may indicate its greater adaptation to an aquatic environment.

INDIAN MARSH CROCODILE (MUGGER)

Crocodylus palustris

DISTRIBUTION: The species is widespread across the Indian subcontinent, from eastern Iran to Sri Lanka. It is found in Pakistan, northern India, the Nepalese lowlands, and Bangladesh. Its numbers are reduced throughout its range because it is hunted for its skin.

HABITAT: The mugger is mainly a freshwater species. Its habitat includes rivers and lakes, and it is also found in reservoirs, water tanks, and irrigation ditches. The largest concentration of this species anywhere is said to be in Hirlan Lake, a reservoir in Gujarat. It has occasionally been sighted in brackish water.

APPEARANCE AND SIZE: Adults are dark grey or brown, with little or no darker banding; juveniles are light brown, with darker crossbands on the tail and spots on the sides of the body. The snout of the adult is short and broad, and the back well-armoured with scales. Indian specimens have four rows of dorsal scutes along the spine, the inner row broader: specimens from Sri Lanka usually have six rows, all of similar width. These southern individuals also have larger and more regular throat scales, giving the appearance of a collar: they may represent a separate subspecies. Adults grow to a maximum of about 5m (16ft).

REPRODUCTION: Females reach sexual maturity at six years, males at ten. The nest is a hole dug into a sandbank above the water line, in which the eggs are buried. The clutch varies from ten to fifty eggs (average: twenty-five). After the eggs have been laid, the hole is covered with a mound of sand or earth about 2m (7ft) in diameter, and up to 1m (3ft 3in) high. Incubation takes fifty to seventy-five days, during which the female guards the nest area. When the eggs are due to hatch, one of the parents digs out the nest in response to faint grunting sounds from the young inside the eggs. Eggs which have not yet hatched are cracked in its jaws by the adult in attendance, and the young are carried to the water.

DIET: Juveniles feed on insects and small vertebrates such as frogs and small fish. Adults take snakes, small mammals and birds, and occasionally raid fishing nets: large specimens have been known to kill deer and even buffalo. In addition there are grisly stories of muggers eating human remains floating down the river after a cremation, which is supposed to give them a taste for human flesh, and turn them into man-eaters. Historical accounts suggest that in previous generations hundreds of people were killed by muggers every year; even if this were true then, there are very few individual muggers living in the wild today which are big enough to offer any real threat to a human.

AMERICAN CROCODILE

Crocodylus acutus

DISTRIBUTION: *C. acutus* is the only crocodile species which is widespread in the Americas. Its range is from southern Florida (mainly in the Everglades and the Florida Keys) to Venezuela, and from the west coast of Mexico to Ecuador and northern Peru. It still occurs on Cuba, Jamaica, and the Cayman Islands, but not in the Bahamas (though subfossil remains have been found there). Across all this range it is now scarce, because of a combination of hunting and habitat destruction.

HABITAT: Freshwater, brackish, and marine habitats are equally suitable for this species, which has salt glands on its tongue similar to those of the saltwater crocodile. In spite of this evidently marine adaptation, it is found high up rivers and in large freshwater lakes. Earlier records of its distribution show that it did not overlap with the Orinoco crocodile or the black caiman, suggesting that direct competition existed between the species. In Panama and Colombia, American crocodiles fed on caimans, which kept away from crocodile habitats as a result. When the crocodiles were hunted out, the caimans invaded all the rivers in which crocodiles used to live.

APPEARANCE AND SIZE: Adults are dark olive above, and pale yellowish below. The skull is convex above the eyes, having a hump which is continued as a ridge about halfway down the rather narrow snout. This is an important characteristic which distinguishes crocodiles from alligators in Florida. In the southern part of the crocodile's range, individuals have a narrower snout than further north. Narrow snouts are associated with fish-eating: perhaps this is an adaptation to an ecological niche which is not accessible to the caimans which are its neighbours. Juveniles are grey-green above, usually with dark cross-markings on the body and tail. The maximum size is about 6m (20ft), with males growing larger than females. There is a record of a 7m (23ft) specimen shot long ago in Venezuela.

REPRODUCTION: The nest may be a hole in the ground, above the high-water mark, or a mound of sand or gravel scraped together among scrub or in mangroves, with a hollow in the top to accommodate the eggs. The clutch size is about thirty-five, and the incubation period about eighty-five days. The female attends the nest, but some reports suggest that she is not very fierce in its defence. Perhaps as a result of intensive hunting, American crocodiles seem to have become very timid, in contrast to their fierce reputation when their habitat was first being settled by humans. The female opens the nest when the young are ready to emerge, and carries the hatchlings to water in her jaws. Both parents guard their young, especially against larger young of their own species, which regard their younger fellows as food.

DIET: Juveniles eat insects when they first hatch, graduating to fish, frogs, and small birds. Adults eat mainly fish, but crabs and water birds are also taken, along with mammals of a suitable size, as large as raccoons or unlucky domestic dogs.

ORINOCO CROCODILE

Crocodylus intermedius

DISTRIBUTION: Limited to the Orinoco Basin in Venezuela, extending along the Meta River to Colombia. Although individuals have been reported from Trinidad, where they must have been carried on rafts of floating vegetation, the species does not live near the sea: at the mouth of the Orinoco, the American crocodile holds sway, either because of its greater adaptation to saline conditions, or because it is fiercer in defending a territory. Like most other crocodiles, the Orinoco crocodile is becoming rare because of hunting: its skin is more valuable than that of the caimans which live in the same region.

HABITAT: The Orinoco crocodile is a freshwater species, preferring slow-flowing rivers or lakes. During the rainy season, when many rivers are in spate, it may wander overland in search of quiet pools. In some areas it is said to pass the dry season in naturally-eroded caves under damp and cool river banks.

APPEARANCE AND SIZE: The Orinoco crocodile is olive-green above, and much paler below. It is another slender-snouted species, rather similar to the American crocodile *C. acutus*, but with a more concave profile, and with the dorsal armour more symmetrically arranged. Some authors have considered that the two species are in fact one, the Orinoco crocodile being a geographical race of *C. acutus*. Juveniles are similar to those of *C. acutus*, with dark cross-bands on a light grey or green background. Under considerable pressure from hunting, adults seldom reach 3m (10ft) nowadays; but there is a record from 1800 of two individuals which were shot by the explorers Humboldt and Bonpland, one measuring 6.7m (22ft) and the other 5.25m (17ft 3in).

REPRODUCTION: The species nests in holes excavated in sandbanks, where it lays its clutch of fifteen to seventy eggs. Incubation takes about six or seven weeks, and the hatchlings when they emerge are guarded by the female for the first few weeks of life. Among the potential predators threatening the eggs and small young are large lizards and black vultures.

DIET: The slender snout of this species suggests that it, too, has evolved to exploit a niche which is not readily available to the caimans. The main diet is fish, with additional birds, amphibians, and small mammals such as capybaras. The Orinoco crocodile has a reputation for attacking humans, but modern specimens probably never grow large enough to be a real threat.

CUBAN CROCODILE

Crocodylus rhombifer

DISTRIBUTION: As its name suggests, the Cuban crocodile lives on the island of Cuba, mainly in the swamps of the Zapata Peninsula. A small population lives on the nearby Isle of Pines. Subfossil remains about 800 years old have been found on Grand Cayman Island, but there are no recent records from anywhere outside Cuba.

HABITAT: With its short toes and only vestigially-webbed feet, the Cuban crocodile is the most land-based living crocodile. It often moves in a 'high walk', and can be seen sitting on its haunches with its forelimbs straight, like a dog. The species lived originally in pools and channels in the interior of freshwater swamps and marshes. It was kept from the coastal fringes by competition with the Cuban population of American crocodiles. However, its hide is too heavily armoured to be much use to the skin trade; as a result, the hunting effort was concentrated on American crocodiles, and the Cuban species was able to colonize the coastal areas once the larger species had been wiped out.

APPEARANCE AND SIZE: This is a very distinctive crocodile, with a short broad snout, and heavily armoured skin, especially along the back and on the hind legs. A pair of bony crests at the back of the skull is sometimes likened to horns. The teeth are slightly splayed outwards in the jaws. Adults are dark grey or black, with yellow spots and larger pale patches. Juveniles are light gold in colour, with black spots and irregular bands on the tail. Adults can grow to as much as 3.5m (11ft 6in), though few attain more than 2m (7ft) nowadays.

REPRODUCTION: Like its close relatives the American crocodile and the Orinoco crocodile, the Cuban species is a hole-nester. Little is known of the details of its breeding behaviour. Juveniles are said to emit a high-pitched alarm call if threatened, which summons adults to their aid; presumably, therefore, there is at least some degree of parental care in this species. Hybrids between the Cuban and American species are often reported, both among captive populations on crocodile farms and in the wild.

DIET: Fish are probably the main item in the diet of the Cuban crocodile, though reports also include waterfowl, turtles and small mammals. The species is notably aggressive towards humans, but because it seldom reaches any great size the victims are more likely to be children than fully-grown adults.

MORELET'S CROCODILE

Crocodylus moreleti

DISTRIBUTION: This species shares most of its range with the American crocodile, from the Caribbean coast of Mexico, across the base of the Yucatan Peninsula, and thence down the coast of Belize to the Peten region of northern Guatemala. In the 1920s it was very numerous around Belize City, but hunting and the destruction of its habitat have reduced its numbers very considerably.

HABITAT: Since its discovery in the 19th century, Morelet's crocodile has been regarded as a strictly freshwater species, living in ponds, lakes, freshwater marshes, and the upper reaches of rivers and streams, as well as in rainforest watercourses. It avoids large, swift rivers. Throughout its range the brackish and salt estuarine areas were occupied by the American crocodile. However, as with the Cuban species, once the American crocodile was severely reduced by over-hunting, Morelet's crocodile showed itself capable of invading the saltier coastal parts of its range.

APPEARANCE AND SIZE: Adults are drab grey-brown on the upper surface, with black spots and bands, and paler underneath. The snout bears a narrow raised ridge, extending nearly to the tip, and the scales protecting the neck are noticeably thickened. Juveniles are spotted in yellow and black. Morelet's crocodile grows to 3.5m (11ft 6in) long.

REPRODUCTION: This species has been closely observed in captivity at Atlanta, Georgia, where it used peat moss and dry leaves to build a mound nest. A clutch of twenty to forty-five eggs was laid in the top of the mound, and covered over by scraping with the hind feet. The female guards the nest until the eggs hatch, after which she carries the hatchlings to water in her jaws, sometimes opening late-hatching eggs in response to sounds from inside. She is occasionally assisted in this task by the male, and there are accounts of parental care by both adults.

DIET: Young Morelet's crocodiles feed on insects caught at the edge of the water, adding snails and slugs to their diet as they grow bigger. Adults also eat snails, along with mud turtles and catfish, as well as small mammals which come to the water to drink. The hindmost teeth in this species are relatively blunt and thick, suggesting that they might be specially developed for crushing the shells of turtles or large molluscs.

NEW GUINEA CROCODILE

Crocodylus novaeguineae

DISTRIBUTION: There is evidence that this is a pair of subspecies (possibly distinct species), with a range of mountains separating them, but since they have not yet been named they must currently be treated as one. *C. novaeguineae* was described in 1928 and reported from the north coast of New Guinea, in the Sepik River drainage. Later, what was thought to be the same species was found on the south coast of Papua, around Lake Murray and the Fly River, on the other side of the Bismarck Range. More recently, morphological studies showed that the two populations are distinct. Reports of a freshwater crocodile from the Irian Jaya region probably refer to the Papuan group. Numbers in the wild fell steadily as a result of hunting, until crocodile farming was introduced in Papua New Guinea in the 1960s, and hunting was much reduced at the same time. The wild population may now be increasing.

HABITAT: This is principally a freshwater species, inhabiting rivers, secluded lakes, marshes and swamps not already colonized by the saltwater crocodile. Where saltwater crocodiles are absent, this species has been seen to enter brackish or coastal habitats for short periods. The Sepik (northern) population extends as high as 600m (650yd) above sea level, in the upper reaches of the August River.

APPEARANCE AND SIZE: Adults are brown, with darker brown or black bands on the tail, and irregular spots on the body. The snout is tapered, but not as slender as that of Johnston's crocodile. Juveniles are pale greenish-yellow above, and much paler underneath, with dark spots on the back arranged into bands which continue on to the tail. Adults can grow to 4m (13ft 2in) long.

REPRODUCTION: Sexual maturity occurs at eight to ten years of age, at a length of about 1.5m (5ft). The Papuan population is said to breed during the wet season, and the Sepik population in the dry. Both build a mound nest from reeds and wet leaves mixed with mud, sometimes on a natural floating platform of grass. The clutch size varies from twenty-three to forty-five eggs. These are laid in a chamber at the top of the mound, which is lined with dry material such as grass and dried leaves. Incubation takes eighty to ninety days, and the female guards the nest throughout that time. Studies have shown that nests built on floating platforms are more likely to fail than those built on dry land (78 per cent compared with 87 per cent). The hatchlings have a yolk sac which can sustain them for up to two weeks without feeding.

DIET: Waterbirds, especially coot and moorhen, form the bulk of the prey, with fish, amphibians and small reptiles making up the rest. Juveniles take insects and small frogs.

PHILIPPINE CROCODILE

Crocodylus mindorensis

DISTRIBUTION: This species is found only in the Philippines, on the islands of Mindoro (where the first specimen was taken), Luzon, Masbate, Samar, Negros, Busuanga, and Mindanao, and on the island of Jolo in the Sulu Archipelago. It was discovered in the central Philippines only in the early 1980s. It may once have been more widespread, but its habitat was destroyed on many islands long ago, during the clearing and formation of agricultural land in the surrounding area.

HABITAT: It is a freshwater species (not, as some have claimed, merely a subspecies of the saltwater crocodile), living in small lakes, the tributaries of large rivers, swamps and marshes. It is very little known, and there is no information about its potential to invade brackish habitats in the local absence of the ubiquitous saltwater crocodile.

APPEARANCE AND SIZE: It has the broadest snout of all the Pacific crocodiles, and a very heavily armoured back and neck. Adults are dull brown, with darker brown or black bands on the tail; the maximum known length is less than 2.5m (8ft 2in).

REPRODUCTION: Very little is known of the breeding habits of this species, save that it is a mound nester, and that there is some degree of parental care.

DIET: Similarly, the diet is not known, but would probably consist of a wide range of prey other than fish. A broad snout in crocodilians is indicative of a generalized diet: turtles, amphibians, and birds from the water, and insects and small mammals from the banks.

SIAMESE CROCODILE

Crocodylus siamensis

DISTRIBUTION: This species was named in 1801 from a specimen collected in Thailand, but it also occurs in Laos, Kampuchea, Vietnam, and the northern part of the Malay peninsula, as well as on some of the Indonesian islands. However, it has been severely over-hunted, for meat as well as skins, and is usually regarded as being practically extinct in its wild habitat. Large stocks are, however, bred on crocodile farms.

HABITAT: This is a palustrine species, inhabiting freshwater lakes, rivers, especially in rainforest, and adjacent marshes. It is not known to make use of estuarine or coastal habitat, but this may well be because its range overlaps with that of the much larger saltwater crocodile.

APPEARANCE AND SIZE: Adults are similar to saltwater crocodiles in appearance, but with a much broader snout, and raised crests behind the eyes rather like the Cuban crocodile. Juveniles are very similar to those of the saltwater crocodile, being golden yellow with black markings. However, unlike the salty, the Siamese crocodile does not exceed 3.5m (11ft 6in) in length.

REPRODUCTION: This species reaches sexual maturity at ten to twelve years. Females build a mound of vegetation, in which they lay twenty to fifty eggs. After an incubation period of about ten weeks, the young within the eggs call to attract their mother's attention, whereupon she opens the nest to release them.

DIET: The main food of the Siamese crocodile is said to be fish; but with its broad snout it would appear to be a generalized feeder, probably taking the usual mixture of amphibians, snakes, insects, and other small prey. Sadly, there is little chance that current knowledge and understanding of the Siamese crocodile will ever be expanded by studies in the wild, since practically the whole of this species now exists only as captive stock, bred on farms for commercial purposes.

JOHNSTON'S CROCODILE

Crocodylus johnsoni

DISTRIBUTION: Johnston's crocodile was named after Robert A. Johnston, who collected the first specimen at Cashmere, Queensland, in the early 1870s. Unfortunately there was a mistake in the documentation of the description, and the rules will not allow a name to be changed once it is established. Thus *johnsoni* is immortalized as a spelling error. Later exploration revealed that the species is found across the northern Australia, from around the Fitzroy River in Western Australia, across the Northern Territory, to Queensland. The type locality is now at or beyond the extreme of its range.

HABITAT: This species occurs mainly in fresh water; in the upper reaches of rivers, and in the pools which result as they break up in the dry season. During the wet season, when large areas of land may be inundated, the crocodiles range widely through forests and grassland. When the dry season starts, they seek deep pools, often returning to one used in previous years from as far as 40km (25 miles) away. In upstream locations, they are said to take shelter in burrows during dry weather. However, there is evidence that they are able to tolerate brackish or even saltwater habitats. In places where saltwater crocodiles have been hunted out, Johnston's crocodiles move closer to the sea, suggesting that their restriction to freshwater is due more to competition than lack of adaptation.

APPEARANCE AND SIZE: Brown in colour and paler underneath, Johnston's crocodile has dark or black bands on the tail, and clear dark bands on the back. The snout is narrow (typical for a freshwater fish-eating species), and the back is well-armoured, with six rows of dorsal scutes. Juveniles are a brighter version of the adults, and very agile, able to gallop like squirrels, a gait used occasionally by adults as well. The maximum length is about 2.5m (8ft 2in) for males, and 2.1m (7ft) for females.

REPRODUCTION: Males mature at thirteen or fourteen years of age (1.8m/6ft long), and females at 11 years (1.5m/5ft). The nest is a hole dug during the dry season in sandy soil or gravel, often on a sandbank away from the shore of a drying creek. Up to eighteen eggs are laid in the moister soil below the surface. The incubation period is ten to twelve weeks, after which the female excavates the nest and carries the hatchlings to water. She guards them for the first month of life. A disturbing feature of the Johnston's crocodile's reproductive cycle is the very high infant mortality rate: it has been estimated that 96 per cent of

The Cuban crocodile is the most terrestrial of all living crocodiles. Its dermal armour is particularly well-developed, its feet have only vestigial webbing, and it uses the 'high walk' more frequently than other species. Its outward-slanting teeth are characteristic of the species. It is notably aggressive towards humans.

hatchlings fail to survive the first two years. Losses are due to predation, in the nest by large lizards and wild pigs, and on the young by birds, large fish, and turtles.
DIET: Johnston's crocodile is a typical freshwater species, using its slender jaws to snap sideways at passing prey, usually fish, crustaceans, and insects. Amphibians, birds, and small mammals are also taken for food when the opportunity arises.

AFRICAN SLENDER-SNOUTED CROCODILE

Crocodylus cataphractus

DISTRIBUTION: This is a tropical forest species, occurring from southern Mauritania and Senegal to northern Angola, and extending eastwards into Zaire, Zambia, and eastern Tanzania. It shares its range throughout with the Nile crocodile.
HABITAT: It is mainly a freshwater species, living in forested rivers and their associated marshes and pools. However, it has been reported from drier savannah country, and also from saltwater lagoons near the coast of Guinea. One specimen was found on Bioko Island, 45km (28 miles) off the coast of Cameroon.
APPEARANCE AND SIZE: The brownish-yellow back is ornamented with large black spots, which are repeated along the lower jaw. The head is grey-green. The slender-snouted crocodile lives up to its name: its jaws are narrow, and smoother than those of other crocodiles. It is especially well-armoured: the thick scales of the neck merge with those of the back, giving a distinctive appearance. (The specific name means 'clad in armour'). Juveniles are pale greenish-grey in colour, with clear black markings. The species grows to 3–4m (10–13ft) in length.
REPRODUCTION: This species builds a mound nest, scraping vegetation together in a shady spot near the bank of a small stream. Clutch sizes reported range from thirteen to twenty-seven eggs. Incubation is about thirteen or fourteen weeks. Breeding is timed so that the hatchlings emerge at the beginning of the wet season. They are thus already quite well-grown when the flooded forest floor makes it easier for them to disperse.
DIET: The African slender-snouted crocodile lives mainly on fish, crabs, shrimps and other small prey, including some water birds.

AFRICAN DWARF CROCODILE

Osteolaemus tetraspis

DISTRIBUTION: This small, slow-moving species lives in the tropical forest zone of west and central Africa, from Senegal to Zaire. It is believed to have been greatly reduced by hunting and the loss of its habitat, until sizeable populations now exist only in forested parts of Senegal, the Central African Republic, Liberia, and Nigeria.
HABITAT: The dwarf crocodile lives in both aquatic forest and savannah, but it prefers slow-moving streams or marshes in rainforest areas. It spends a large part of its time on land, and is apparently at least partly nocturnal. Unlike other crocodiles, it does not spend long periods basking in the sun, preferring to pass the day in shady places or in holes in the banks of streams.
APPEARANCE AND SIZE: Adults are dark in colour all over. This is a heavily armoured species: the armour is especially heavy round the large eyes, continuing over the head and neck and down the back, where there are six or eight rows of tough scutes. Even the belly and throat bear thickened plates. The snout is very short, and the eyes very large, giving a juvenile appearance even to the adults. Actual juveniles are brown, spotted with black above, with black bars on the body and tail, and black and yellow plates below. The species grows to less than 2m (7ft) in length.
REPRODUCTION: The dwarf crocodile is a mound nester, using damp vegetation to build a structure about 1.5m (5ft) across. The clutch size is ten to twenty eggs, and the incubation period is about sixteen weeks. Newly emerged hatchlings are tiny: they weigh little more than 50gm (2oz).
DIET: The diet is very poorly documented, but is reported to consist of crabs, frogs, and fish.

ALLIGATORS AND CAIMANS
Subfamily Alligatorinae

AMERICAN ALLIGATOR

Alligator mississippiensis

DISTRIBUTION: The American alligator is found only in the United States, along the Atlantic coastal plain from the borders of Virginia and North Carolina south round Florida to the eastern Texas coast near the Rio Grande. It extends inland up the Mississippi River drainage as far as southern Arkansas and Oklahoma. In parts of Texas it is expanding its range by making use of water holes dug for cattle.

HABITAT: The American alligator is principally a palustrine species, adapted to living in marshes and swamps; however, it lives also in rivers and lakes, brackish estuarine areas, and even in salt water at the coast. It is particularly conspicuous in Florida in areas which have been drained for building, apparently settling contentedly into ornamental pools left among the housing plots, where it causes consternation among the house-owners.

APPEARANCE AND SIZE: The back of the adult is a very dark greenish-grey, with no visible cross-markings in fully adult animals. Juveniles vary in colour, but the ground colour is black, with bold stripes of pale yellow (in the western part of the range) or yellow-brown (in the east). These crossbands fade as the animal grows older. The head is massive, with a broad snout having a decidedly more concave shape than that of the American crocodile. In the past, specimens were shot which were more than 6m (20ft) long, but today an adult male of 4m (13ft 2in) is considered large.

REPRODUCTION: The reproduction of the American alligator has been intensively studied, during various campaigns either to control or to preserve populations of the animal. It is a mound nester, the female building a heap of plant material in a spot chosen for its safety from flooding or drying out. Nests are usually in the shade of dense vegetation, often under trees on a raised part of the swamp. The eggs are laid in a hollow in the top of the mound; the clutch size is between thirty and fifty-five, with older females laying more eggs than young ones. The female guards the nest for the whole of the incubation period, leaving it only for brief feeding trips. She will charge, hissing, at intruders, attacking smaller animals such as raccoons (which frequently raid nests while the female is away), but usually backing down at the last minute if the intruder is a human. The eggs hatch after nine or ten weeks, or a little more quickly in warmer weather. The nest temperature determines the sex of the hatchlings: below 30°C (86°F), only females are produced, while over 34°C (93°F), all the hatchlings are males. At temperatures in between, the sexes are mixed.

The American alligator's maternal care of its eggs and young was rumoured from early times, but it was not documented until 1978, when the scientist James Kushlan and the photographer Jeff Simon were making a film in Florida for the *Survival* series on British television. Since then, it has become very well known, and is also recorded for a number of other crocodilian species. The female lifts eggs which are ready to hatch, and rolls them between her teeth until the shell cracks. She then carries the hatchling in her jaws to a nearby canal or pond, or sometimes to a pool which she has dug near the nest for the purpose. Reaching the water, she backs in, and opens her jaws wide enough for the baby to swim out. Maternal care continues for as long as three years, or sometimes four, the mother responding to distress calls from smaller youngsters by rushing to their rescue.

DIET: Juveniles begin feeding about three days after hatching, when the yolk sac is used up. They start by grubbing in the bottom sediment for morsels of anything edible, graduating as they grow to a larger range of prey. Even quite large animals are found with insects in their stomachs, alongside frogs, snakes, turtles, and birds. Alligators were filmed by Jeff Simon leaping clear of the water to catch herons sitting on branches above them. Fully-grown adults can take raccoons, calves, and occasionally humans.

CHINESE ALLIGATOR

Alligator sinensis

DISTRIBUTION: Today, the Chinese alligator lives in a rather restricted area of the lower Chang Chiang (Yangtze) basin, inland from Shanghai, between T'ai Hu (Lake Tai) and the main course of the river. In historical times it was much more widespread, covering the whole of the middle and most of the upper Yangtze, extending nearly to 110° west, and reaching to the upper drainage of the Yellow River (about 35° north). However, this part of China is very densely populated, and the alligator was forced to retreat before the pressure of agricultural and urban development.

HABITAT: The area where the alligator survives is flooded every summer, producing marshland with numerous ponds and lakes. This is an ideal habitat for the species, and, more importantly for its survival, it is land which is unsuitable for farming, so that the alligator has its home to itself. There

The muggers of Sri Lanka are often classified as a distinct subspecies, having a collar of broad plates round the neck, and six rows of dorsal scutes instead of four.

are groups of alligators living in the hill country, in pools as much as 100m above sea level, where there are fewer people but plentiful food resources. The species is mainly nocturnal, having been persecuted by humans for many centuries, and it spends most of the day lying-up in a burrow. During the winter months (October to March) it hibernates in the same burrow.

APPEARANCE AND SIZE: At first sight, the Chinese alligator looks like a small version of the American alligator, to which it is very closely related. Adults are greenish-black on the back, with yellow streaks and spots on the sides, and grey underneath. There are several subtle differences from the American species: the eyelids have a bony plate, the head is more robust, and the snout is very broad and noticeably upturned. Juveniles are black, like those of the American alligator, but with fewer yellow stripes. In Chinese literature dating back to the seventh century BC alligators are said to reach 3m (10ft) in length, but today they seldom exceed 1.5m (5ft), which includes even the examples in museum collections.

REPRODUCTION: Sexual maturity occurs at four or five years of age. The nest is a mound of grass and dry leaves, built in June or July. The eggs, ten to forty in number, are laid in the mound in much the same way as those of the American alligator. Incubation takes ten weeks. There is no record of maternal care of the young, but this might be because the species has not been studied closely enough in the wild.

DIET: The sturdy jaws and rounded rear teeth of the Chinese alligator suggest that it is adapted to crushing hard objects. Its diet is known to include snails and clams, and probably also the terrapins which are common in its habitat. The young eat insects and other small invertebrates, and the stomach contents of older animals have been found to include the remains of rats. The species is too small and timid to pose any threat to humans.

SPECTACLED CAIMAN

Caiman crocodilus

DISTRIBUTION: This species gets its name from the bony ridges surrounding each eye socket, and the transverse ridge connecting them, giving the impression of eyeglasses. It has a very wide range, from southern Mexico to subtropical South America, close to the border between Paraguay and Argentina. It consists of three (or six) subspecies, which are given separate names. In the north the brown caiman, *C. crocodilus fuscus*, extends from southern Mexico to Venezuela, Colombia, and Ecuador; the common caiman, *C. crocodilus crocodilus*, occurs east of the Andes from Venezuela to the Amazon basin as far as Brazil; and the jacare, *C. crocodilus yacare*, lives in the Mato Grosso. Two other subspecies, *paraguayensis* and *matogrossoensis*, occur within the range of the jacare, and there is another, *apaporiensis*, found in a very short stretch of the River Apaporo in Colombia. For the purposes of this list, they will all be considered together as spectacled caimans.

HABITAT: Spectacled caimans are very adaptable, and as a result they have suffered less than other crocodilians from human alterations to their habitat. They can live in virtually all open areas, such as swamps, savannahs, lakes and rivers; they prefer slow-moving or still water to swift rivers, and sun to shade. They have been found in cattle ponds, reservoirs, and even roadside borrow pits. The common caiman is tolerant of salt water, and has reached Trinidad.

APPEARANCE AND SIZE: Adults are grey-green on the back, and paler below, with dark bands on the tail. The 'spectacles' which give the species its common name have already been described. Subspecies vary in colour, sometimes from one end to the other of their range: the brown caiman is brown in the north, but olive-green in the south. Juveniles are also variable, but the standard design is a yellowish-brown background, with black crossbands around the body and tail.

REPRODUCTION: Spectacled caimans build mound nests of earth mixed with leaf litter and fallen leaves and twigs. They lay between fifteen and forty eggs, depending on the size and age of the female, the average being twenty-five to thirty. Incubation takes ten to twelve weeks. The male is said to open the nest, and to crack the eggs with his jaws to release the hatchlings, while the female waits for them in the water nearby.

DIET: Small babies feed on water beetles, graduating to crabs, water snails, and small fish. Adults eat catfish and carrion of all kinds during the dry season, and small deer and pigs, but mainly fish, during the wet season. There is a common myth that caimans reduce populations of water snails so much that the snails cannot act as intermediate hosts for human parasites. This is untrue: waters with large caiman populations usually contain especially large populations of snails, feeding on the lush growth of water plants fed by the caimans' droppings.

BLACK CAIMAN

Melanosuchus niger

DISTRIBUTION: The black caiman is found throughout the Amazon basin, and it may from time to time reach Guyana by way of rivers flowing northwards. Its population is now much reduced throughout this range by hunting for skins.
HABITAT: The black caiman has become a retiring species as a result of hunting. Its habitat in earlier days was often beaches and other open places, but now it is to be found in lakes and sluggish rivers deep in the flooded forest. Juveniles may still be seen near floating grass mats in open water, but if they survive they seek out more secluded places when they are bigger.
APPEARANCE AND SIZE: The black caiman is, not surprisingly, mainly black, with paler yellowish underparts. Its head is paler brown, with dark blotches. The head is broad, tapering to a rather sharp snout. Juveniles are deep black, with light grey heads, and rows of white or yellow dots forming broken crossbands on the body. In the past, adults reached a length of 6m (20ft), making them the largest predators on the South American continent; but today 4.5m (14ft 8in) would be a very large black caiman.
REPRODUCTION: The nest is a mound of vegetation similar to that of the American alligator, but usually much larger. Thirty to sixty eggs are laid, and the incubation period is about six weeks.
DIET: Black caimans feed mostly at night; they have very sharp sight and hearing. Juveniles feed on insects, and the usual invertebrate young-crocodilian diet. Adults eat fish during the dry season, when they are concentrated by the falling water level into small pools; but the principal prey of larger individuals in the wet season is capybaras, rodents which are numerous in the Amazon forests. An unexpected problem caused by the severe reduction in the black caiman population was an explosion of capybaras, their population no longer controlled by predation. Crops in jungle villages were destroyed by the marauding rodents. Another side-effect occurred in the water: without caiman droppings to feed on, the plankton content fell, and the fish fry which used to feed on plant and animal plankton failed to mature. Some fish species are now greatly reduced as a result — with one exception. Some species of piranha, which used to be heavily predated by black caimans, are now so numerous that it is dangerous to allow cattle into the flooded pastures where the fish congregate. The black caiman is the only caiman species which is regarded as dangerous to humans, but reports of attacks on humans are very few.

BROAD-SNOUTED CAIMAN

Caiman latirostris

DISTRIBUTION: This species is restricted to the eastern part of South America, from Rio Grande do Norte, in Brazil, to Uruguay. It occurs inland along rivers as far south as the Rio Paraguay in Argentina.
HABITAT: The broad-snouted caiman is found most often in shallow freshwater swamps, or streams with densely-vegetated banks, but also in mangroves along large rivers and round the edges of lakes. It is also able to live in brackish or salt water.
APPEARANCE AND SIZE: The broad-snouted caiman is dark greenish on the back, with a yellow belly. The tail is paler, with dark bands. It has a broad, heavy-looking head, with a ridged muzzle. Adults seldom exceed 3m (10ft) in length in the north of the range; in the south, the maximum length recorded is 1.8m (5ft 10in).
REPRODUCTION: The nest is a mound of decaying vegetation, built near water by the female. There are between thirty and sixty eggs, which take eight to twelve weeks to hatch. The female defends the nest throughout incubation, and both parents care for the young for the first year of life.
DIET: Juveniles eat insects and crustaceans, and adults feed on snails, crabs, and only occasionally on small vertebrates such as lizards, rodents and birds.

SCHNEIDER'S DWARF CAIMAN

Palaeosuchus trigonatus

DISTRIBUTION: *P. trigonatus* lives in the tropical rainforests of the Amazon and Orinoco basins, as well as in Guyana, French Guyana, and Surinam. This miniature species is

probably the most abundant crocodilian in the world today.
HABITAT: Dwarf caimans live in small streams in forests with a closed canopy. They do not bask, and spend a large part of their time away from water, often hiding under fallen debris or in hollow logs as much as 50m (55yd) from the stream.
APPEARANCE AND SIZE: Dwarf caimans may be an ancient offshoot from the main body of crocodilians, having many primitive features. Their name means 'ancient crocodile'. On the other hand, some of their characteristics may be adaptations to life in the dense forest. Schneider's is dark in colour, with a very heavily armoured skin: the scutes on the neck and tail are said to be so sharp that it is difficult to hold a struggling animal. Both species lack the 'spectacles' of other caimans — hence their alternative name, which is 'smooth-fronted caimans'. Male Schneider's dwarf caimans reach about 1.7m (5ft 8in) in length, females no more than 1.4m (4ft 7in).
REPRODUCTION: Females become sexually mature at 1.3m (4ft 4in) in length, males at 1.4 (4ft 7in). The mound nest is made at the end of the dry season, and the clutch of ten to fifteen eggs hatches at the beginning of the rainy season, twelve to thirteen weeks later.
DIET: Because of its partly terrestrial habit, Schneider's dwarf caiman eats less fish or snails than other caimans: its main diet is snakes, birds, and lizards, and mammals such as porcupines and rodents. Juveniles start life eating insects, but quickly graduate to the adult diet.

CUVIER'S DWARF CAIMAN

Palaeosuchus palpebrosus

DISTRIBUTION: Cuvier's dwarf caiman covers the same range as Schneider's, with an extension southwards along the Paraguay and Parana Rivers. It is as widely distributed as the common caiman, but at much lower densities.
HABITAT: This species differs from Schneider's in that it occurs more often around lake shores in the forest, and less along small streams. It basks in the sun with its head up, often on slabs of rock away from the shore. Its rusty colour probably serves as camouflage in water covered with floating dead leaves.
APPEARANCE AND SIZE: Adults are light brown in colour, with a gingery or rusty coloured head, which is heavily armoured. The head is shorter and broader than that of *P. trigonatus*, with a blunt, upturned snout. Juveniles have a yellowish-brown head, with the lower jaw light brown, and black or dark brown crossbands on body and tail. Adult males grow to about 1.5m (5ft), females to 1.2m (4ft).
REPRODUCTION: Cuvier's dwarf caiman has been studied in some detail, so that its nesting habits are better known than Schneider's. The mound nest is built with damp, rotting material, mixed with twigs and mud, in a shady place. Ten to twelve eggs are laid in a chamber at the top of the mound, where the rotting vegetation keeps the temperature somewhat higher than that of the surrounding air.

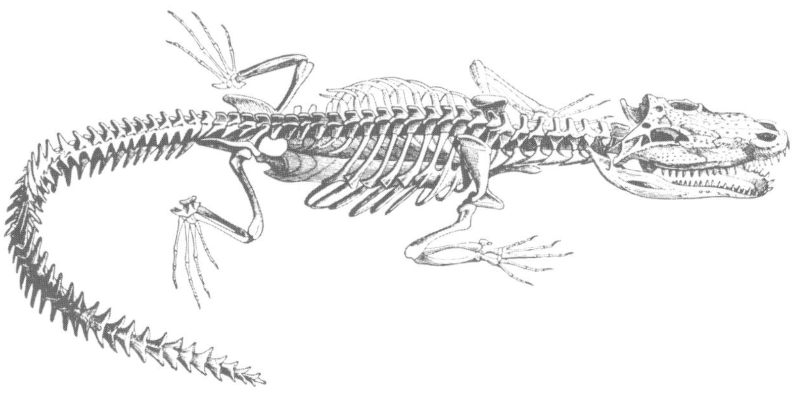

The incubation period is about twelve to thirteen weeks. The female digs the eggs out when they are ready to hatch; there is no record of parental defence in this species, but it may well occur.
DIET: Cuvier's dwarf caiman eats very much the same diet as Schneider's, but there is good evidence that it is a cannibal. The remains of juveniles of both species have been found in its stomach.

GAVIAL
Subfamily Gavialinae

GAVIAL

Gavialis gangeticus

DISTRIBUTION: The gavial (or gharial) once lived all round the world: fossil relatives have been found in South and North America, Africa and Asia. The modern species lived in a range extending originally from Pakistan to Burma across the top of the Indian subcontinent, but is now restricted to two main locations. One is in the Indus in the west, and another larger, group lives in the east, in the rivers Ganges (in India and southern Nepal) and Brahmaputra, (in Bangladesh and Assam).

HABITAT: The gavial lives in deep, fast-flowing rivers as well as the broader, shallower tributaries of the Ganges in the Nepalese terai.

APPEARANCE AND SIZE: Adults are light in colour, ranging from olive to tan, with dark bands and blotches on body and tail. The long, parallel-sided snout is often held at a raised angle when the animal is basking. The rear feet are fully webbed, and its legs are weak, making it sluggish on land. Juveniles are plain dark brown, and about 36cm (14in) long when they first hatch. A day later, they fade to pale brown. Adults grow to 6m (20ft) in length; the largest on record, shot in 1924, was 7m (23ft) long.

REPRODUCTION: The nest is a hole dug into a sandy bank or a sandbank in mid-river, not more than 10m (33ft) from the water. The clutch is usually twenty-five to forty-five eggs, though one nest in 1982 had ninety-seven, of which sixty-nine hatched. Incubation takes between nine and thirteen weeks, the female guarding the nest from potential predators such as jackals and monitor lizards. The parents open the nest in response to calls from the hatching young.

DIET: Gavials eat fish almost exclusively, snapping sideways at passing schools. Their favoured food is catfish, which are in their turn predators on the commercially important tilapia. The steep decline in gavials since the 1950s has allowed catfish to flourish, causing harm to the tilapia catch, and hardship to the villagers who depend on them for survival.

FALSE GAVIAL
Subfamily Thoracosaurinae

FALSE GAVIAL

Tomistoma schlegeli

DISTRIBUTION: The false gavial is found on the Malay Peninsula, in southern Thailand, Borneo and Sumatra. Subfossil remains from China indicate that it occurred there in historical times, perhaps as recently as the seventeenth century.

HABITAT: *Tomistoma* is found in freshwater swamps, lakes and rivers. There are no records from brackish or marine habitats. Captive animals dig burrows in which they hide, though this has not been seen in the wild.

APPEARANCE AND SIZE: Adults are dark in colour, with broad black bands on the tail, and black bands and blotches on the body and head. The false gavial lacks the sharp demarcation between skull and snout which gives the gavial its distinctive appearance. In *Tomistoma*, the head tapers gradually to form the long, slender snout. Juveniles are similarly marked. Adults grow to as much as 5m (16ft 5in) in length.

REPRODUCTION: Females are sexually mature at about five years old, when they are 3m (10ft) in length. The nest, a mound of dead leaves, is built near water, in a shady place. Twenty to sixty eggs are laid, and the incubation time is ten to twelve weeks. Apparently the parents do not help the hatchlings to escape from the eggs, and there is no account of parental care after hatching.

DIET: The appearance of the false gavial suggests that it feeds on fish like the gavial, but there are accounts of it taking monkeys from the banks of streams, and the remains of other small vertebrates have been found in its stomach. The diet may be broader than was previously thought.

LEGENDS AND TRUTH

CROCODILE TEARS

Crocodiles cannot cry. The myth of their tears, supposedly shed to induce pity in the beholder, thus enticing him to come within range of the jaws, arose from an account by Sir

James Hawkins, the explorer. In 1565 he returned from a visit to the New World, reporting that there were 'many Crocodils' there, and that they 'cry and sobbe' to achieve their nefarious ends. From this, poets and philosophers developed the idea of false grief to evoke pity, followed by false remorse. Thus did a phrase and a body of ideas come into the language, based on nothing more than a mistaken interpretation of the warning roar of an alligator.

CROCODILE MAGIC

The white hunter Frederick Courteney Selous, writing in 1881, told of his companion shooting a large crocodile in one of the tributaries of the Zambesi. He warned the man not to let the fact be known to the local Matabele, because they were 'very superstitious about the animal, believing that any one possessed of its liver is able to bewitch other people, and play the devil generally'. The Thonga tribe in northern Zululand believe the liver to be poisonous — which it is, if it is allowed to decompose slightly — and insist that the liver of an animal killed by a hunter be publicly burned, to protect the rest of the tribe from mischief.

Elsewhere in Africa, crocodiles are believed to be the incarnation of the spirits of the dead, often benevolent guardians of the villages where they had lived. Boys would call the animals by name, summoning them to receive offerings of food. In Uganda the food was sometimes the enemies of the tribe, captured in battle, but more often it was a symbolic morsel offered by the villagers to keep on the right side of the crocodile.

Also in Uganda, and independently in Madagascar, crocodiles were used in trials by ordeal. The accused was taken to the bank of a river where crocodiles lived, and after the facts of the case had been announced to the animals, forced to cross. If the crocodiles took the man, he was guilty.

There are tribes which regard the crocodile as a benevolent neighbour; one such is the Nuer, in the Nile valley. They calmly waded through crocodile-infested streams with the explorer Evans–Pritchard, explaining that there was no danger, because the people who lived nearby had the crocodile as their totem. Elsewhere, a tooth or a claw from a crocodile, preferably one which is known to have killed cattle or people, renders the wearer immune from attack by crocodiles.

REVENGE

In many countries where crocodiles are common, the risk of attack is accepted, if not with equanimity, at least fatalistically. There are some cultures where, although the crocodile is venerated, it is from time to time necessary to punish an individual animal for wrong-doing. The Dayak of Borneo, for example, refrain from killing crocodiles: but if the parents of a child which has been taken by one insist — and pay the right price — the village magician will set out to kill crocodiles in the area, slitting open their bellies until he finds the remains of the child. The whole village will then make a sacrifice, usually a cat, to the surviving crocodiles, to atone for the slaughter of the innocent animals.

In countries colonized by Europeans, large crocodilians were objects of terror. There must have been many deaths in African rivers, the swamps of Louisiana, and northern parts of Australia among early settlers. Unlike the natives, the new arrivals had firearms, and could easily kill the sluggish animals. At first, no doubt, they killed crocodiles to exact revenge; but it cannot have been long before they began to slaughter them pre-emptively.

The 'sport' of shooting caimans from river boats in South American countries wiped out local populations in many places where natives and crocodilians had lived side by side for thousands of years. The 'hunters' no doubt thought that they were doing good, and making the country safer. They did not even attempt to collect the hides (there was no organized trade in them at the time), but left the corpses to rot on the river bank. In fact, far from doing good, by wiping out the black caiman over much of its range, for example, they damaged the local fishery and boosted the population of piranhas to a dangerous level.

MAN-EATERS

Marco Polo, returning from China in the thirteenth century, described the Chinese alligator in terms that were guaranteed to set his hearers' hair on end. They were hideous, voracious man-eaters, according to his account, and 'every man and beast must stand in fear and trembling of them'. He was wrong, as we now know: the Chinese alligator may be no beauty, but in fact it is shy and non-aggressive towards humans.

Some middle-sized species occasionally attack or even prey on humans. American alligators, black caimans, Orinoco crocodiles, and muggers have all been documented as attacking from time to time. The American crocodile is noted for its aggressive behaviour, but in all of these species attacks on humans are rare.

There are only two species which may accurately be called man-eaters: the Nile crocodile, and the saltwater crocodile. The latter has been described as the only reptile which regularly treats man as a prey animal. Both species grow to a large size, and both are found over large inhabited areas of the world. Their behaviour has had a malign influence in the way in which humans view all crocodilians.

ATTACKS BY NILE CROCODILES

A Nile crocodile has numerous enemies and competitors in the wild, including members of its own species. Nest predators range from lizards and jackals to humans, and the young crocodiles are prey to large fish, birds, and other crocodiles. Furthermore, the Nile crocodile lives among a wide variety of potential prey animals, including large mammals which it can catch while they are drinking. Consequently, it is not only very defensive of its nest and young, but also aggressive towards anything which might form a meal. Humans entering the crocodile's realm do so on the crocodile's terms.

Native people who live in crocodile country learn to take certain precautions against being attacked; their small boats are vulnerable, and they themselves are in danger whenever they go to the river bank to wash or to fetch water. Visitors to such areas from the cities, or from overseas, are often unaware of the danger. Not knowing how silently and suddenly an attack might come, they are off their guard. A number of fatalities result from the carelessness brought about by ignorance.

A crocodile lying motionless in muddy water, among reeds or water lilies, is very hard to see. Its eyes, ears and nostrils are all that show above the surface. Prey animals or potential enemies, including people, may approach to within a few feet without knowing the crocodile is there. By the time they find out, it is too late.

If a crocodile spots a potential victim from some way out in the water, it will submerge and swim stealthily towards the bank, making a mighty lunge at the last moment, often travelling some way up the bank with the momentum of the attack. A full-sized adult may weigh 1000kg (2250lb), and will have killed animals as large as wildebeeste or buffalo: a puny human would stand no chance of survival.

The most dangerous time to be in crocodile country is during the breeding season, when adult males are defending their territories, and both sexes are guarding nests. In a study of forty-three attacks in northern Zululand and southern Mozambique, it was found that thirty-nine of them took place during the breeding season, between November and April. Many were by small, possibly sub-adult, crocodiles, about 2.5m (8ft 2in) long and weighing 100kg (225lb): these were seldom fatal, though the victims sustained serious injuries, including the loss of hands or feet, lacerations, and broken limbs. Larger crocodiles were able to kill partly from the shock of the impact, but mainly because they could inflict larger injuries more quickly, and drag their victims into the water to drown them.

ATTACKS BY SALTWATER CROCODILES

Most of the Nile crocodile's attacks are connected with

American alligators rarely attack humans. There have been one or two recent assaults on small children in Florida, and occasional reports of alligators stalking fishermen – probably because the reptiles have lost their fear of humans now that they are protected – but no fatalities for many years.

defending its nest or its territory, but those of the saltwater crocodile are more often predatory. In villages in south-eastern Asia, crocodiles have always been a regular cause of death; and, as in Africa, visitors from cities are unaware of their danger. The success of the film *Crocodile Dundee*, and the insouciance of its central character, did little to reduce the incidence of crocodile attacks in northern Australia. It may have increased the risk, by encouraging a macho attitude towards the danger.

Saltwater crocodiles have been known to take people only ankle-deep in water. Fishermen have even been taken from river banks a metre or more above the water. To elect to bathe or swim in creeks or from beaches where crocodiles are known to occur is potentially suicidal. In view of the obvious danger, it is surprising that between 1975 and 1988 there were only twelve fatalities from crocodiles in northern Australia. Several times that number of people were attacked, but survived.

CONSERVATION OF CROCODILIANS

CROCODILES IN DANGER

The commercial hunting of crocodilians for their skins started only in the mid-nineteenth century, when the quality of the leather was recognised in countries with colonies in which crocodilians were abundant. Before then, hunting had been at a relatively low level, mainly by native peoples for food or for ritual purposes, or by white settlers out of fear and loathing. Although this latter pressure had a severe effect on some populations, such as that of the black caiman, it was the commercial hunting which did serious damage to crocodilian populations world wide.

Seventeen species or subspecies of crocodilians are listed as endangered in appendices to CITES (the Convention on International Trade in Endangered Species). Only five species, the American alligator, both dwarf caimans, Johnston's crocodile, and the New Guinea crocodile, are not at present endangered. Parts of some populations may still be hunted, for example the Nile crocodile in Zimbabwe and some other African countries, or the saltwater crocodile in Australia and Papua New Guinea. In other territories, hunting is permitted under an annual quota designed to restrict the harvest to sustainable levels.

CROCODILES AND TRADE

Many countries with endemic crocodile populations are making attempts to manage the trade, often by developing a complete industry within the country, from breeding and rearing the animals through to marketing the products made with their skins. The principal problem with this approach is that there will always exist a market for skins taken from the wild, alongside the legitimate market. Research is still going on into ways of marking or identifying in some other way skins which have come from captive-bred animals.

A halfway house to this position is rearing eggs collected from nests in the wild. In countries where this is common, crocodile-rearing concerns are supposed to return a percentage of the grown animals to the wild, to support the natural population. This is very difficult to enforce.

The single largest exporter of crocodile skins is Papua New Guinea, which supplies about 40 per cent of the legal world market. (75 per cent of the total market consists of skins of the common caiman, most of them taken illegally.) There, both saltwater and New Guinea crocodiles are hunted under carefully controlled quotas, covering both the number and the size of animals which may be taken. Increasingly, crocodiles are bred in captivity, and the annual harvest from the wild is reduced to keep the total supply of skins at a level which maintains prices on the world market. Crocodile ranching is a growing business in northern Australia, where there are at least eight major crocodile farms.

THE CROCODILE BANK

The Madras Crocodile Bank was founded in 1975. It began with fourteen muggers, but now has a stock of 3,550 crocodiles of ten different species, in more than four hectares of land. The Bank was founded by Romulus Whitaker, an American who grew up in India, with a grant from the Worldwide Fund for Nature. Funds today come from a variety of sources, including branches of the leather industry. The breeding has been so successful that the Bank now has a problem with the number of crocodiles on its premises. They have released over 500 muggers into the wild in places where they had become scarce, or to other breeding centres, but they still have a stock of nearly 3,000, descended from the original fourteen. Half a million visitors a year come to see the crocodiles, contributing to the Bank's important work of public education.

A concerted effort by the Food and Agriculture Organization of the United Nations Development Programme has succeeded in restoring the fortunes of the gavial in India. The population in the mid-seventies was barely thirty animals, partly because of hunting, but also as a result of habitat degradation. By rearing hatchlings from eggs collected from the wild, and releasing them into restored and protected areas when they were big enough to fend for themselves, the FAO/UNDP project has raised the wild population to more than 3,000.

THE FUTURE FOR CROCODILIANS

Immense progress has been made in controlling the trade in crocodile skins, and in encouraging farming, captive breeding, and other methods of limiting the rate at which animals are taken from the wild. However, captive breeding is not enough to maintain the genetic diversity of populations, because all too often all the animals on a farm are descended from a small initial stock. The other arm of the conservation effort is to restore wild habitat in places where it has been degraded or destroyed by human activities. This requires the establishment of a network of nature reserves and national parks. Some countries have made good progress along this road, but there remains a good deal to be done.

A serious handicap in crocodile conservation is that crocodiles are not pandas. They cannot in any terms be considered cuddly. There are still countries where they are not only loathed but officially classified as vermin.

After a series of human fatalities in Queensland, Australia, in 1985 and 1986, fishermen were shooting saltwater crocodiles on sight, in spite of the fact that it was illegal to kill them. The local Minister of the Environment stated publicly that he wanted crocodiles completely wiped out.

In Madagascar, where the conservation of lemurs is making good progress, Nile crocodiles are still a vermin species, according to legislation passed in 1962, apparently not repealed. They have become very scarce since the mid-1950s, when they were widespread and reasonably abundant in the Betsiboka River. The most recent report of the International Union for the Conservation of Nature calls them 'very diffuse and rare'. In the light of this, it is hard to understand how the 1985 CITES meeting was able to move them from Appendix I (endangered) to Appendix II (not at present endangered), thus permitting legal trade in their skins. An annual quota of 1,000 skins was established: but no-one knows whether there are as many as 1,000 Nile crocodiles left in this fascinating isolated population.

LET THE SURVIVORS SURVIVE

Crocodilians survived from the age of the dinosaurs into our own, as the sole remaining archosaurs. They throw light on our studies of animals long since fossilized, and of an age before birds and mammals, let alone man, were seen on earth. All over their range they are threatened by human activities, especially by hunting for skins, but also by the degradation of their habitat and by slaughter driven by fear and hatred. There are those who would say that this is an extension of natural selection, that the crocodilians have had their day and are not equipped to survive in a modern world. The answer to this is that in most of the places where they live, crocodilians are an essential part of the local ecosystem — remember the black caiman.

Another answer is that animals which have survived the greatest catastrophes the world has seen, the Cretaceous extinction and a series of Ice Ages, have every right to survive the impact of a small bipedal mammal which prides itself on being the only species ever to have evolved a conscience.

EXAMPLES OF VARIOUS SPECIES

American alligator

Nile crocodile

Indian Marsh crocodile (mugger)

Johnston's crocodile

Siamese crocodile

New Guinea crocodile

Cuban crocodile

Morelet's crocodile

Chinese alligator

Orinoco crocodile

Spectacled caiman

African Dwarf crocodile

Gavial

American crocodile

False gavial

REPRODUCTION, BIRTH & YOUNG

Contrary to their fearsome reputation – some of which is justified, but just as much of which arises from too ready a belief in apocryphal folk stories and exaggerated traveller's tales – crocodilians are remarkably gentle and caring in both their courtship and mating rituals, and in their maternalism and rearing habits.

The photographs in this section illustrate the serenity, for example, with which male and female Nile crocodiles come together in the slowly moving river – admittedly after the male has performed a highly aggressive dominance display to see off lesser rivals and claim the female of his choice.

Similarly the mother crocodilian's concern for her young is examined: her care in nest-building and watching over her young for periods of up to four years — during a period when the off-spring are highly vulnerable to many predators including their crocodilian elders — is reminiscent of the meticulous maternalism of many bird-types, with whom crocodilians, of course, share a common heritage, albeit many thousands of years ago.

OPPOSITE PAGE

The care shown by female alligators for their young, lasting sometimes for as long as four years, appears to be in sharp contrast to the animals' fierce reputation. It should not seem so surprising: crocodilians and birds (who are excellent parents) share a common ancestry.

Courtship among Nile crocodiles can be a surprisingly gentle business. It usually takes place in the early afternoon, after a morning of basking. After initial tussles (above), in which any rival males are driven away from the prospective mate, the dominant male lies alongside the female in the water, pressing his body against hers with sinuous movements (opposite top), and rubbing the underside of his jaws across the female's neck (opposite middle). Mating can take place only with her co-operation (opposite below). The male grips her with his claws while they mate for about two minutes. The dominant male will copulate with most of the females in the community. He can mate several times in the course of a single afternoon, at intervals of about an hour.

ABOVE

American alligators mating. Copulation is preceded by protracted courtship, in which the male strokes the female with a forefoot, and rubs her neck with his throat, producing a scent from his throat glands which stimulates the female.

LEFT

A female mugger often initiates courtship by swimming round the male with her head raised. He may respond by rubbing the underside of his jaws on her head and body. Mating begins on the surface, but often finishes underwater.

A male gavial's snout has a bulbous structure at the end the function of which has never been determined. It is unlikely to be connected with breathing or a sense of smell, since it cannot be closed against the water, and it contains no apparent specialized sense-cells. One theory is that is serves as a resonator used by males in courtship.

When her eggs are close to hatching, about seventy days after they were laid, a female Chinese alligator clears away the leaves and twigs on top of the nest mound to expose the eggs. The hatchlings are 20cm (8in) long, and between ten and forty in number. Their bright coloration is an effective camouflage in mottled light. They will become sexually mature at four or five years old.

New Guinea crocodiles hatch after an incubation of eighty to ninety days. They do not need to feed for the first two to fourteen days because they carry a residual yolk sac which sustains them. Their temperature at this time is high; it falls from 34°C (93°F) to around 32°C (90°F) when normal feeding begins.

Young alligators tend to stay in groups of their own size, for fear of the aggression of larger animals, especially territorial males.

American alligators may be protected by their mothers for as long as four years after they hatch. By the time their cross-bands are fading, the young alligators are too big to be taken by predators, and ready to take their place in adult society.

The bright colours of a first-year American alligator serve as surprisingly effective camouflage in the swamps where it lives under its mother's protection.

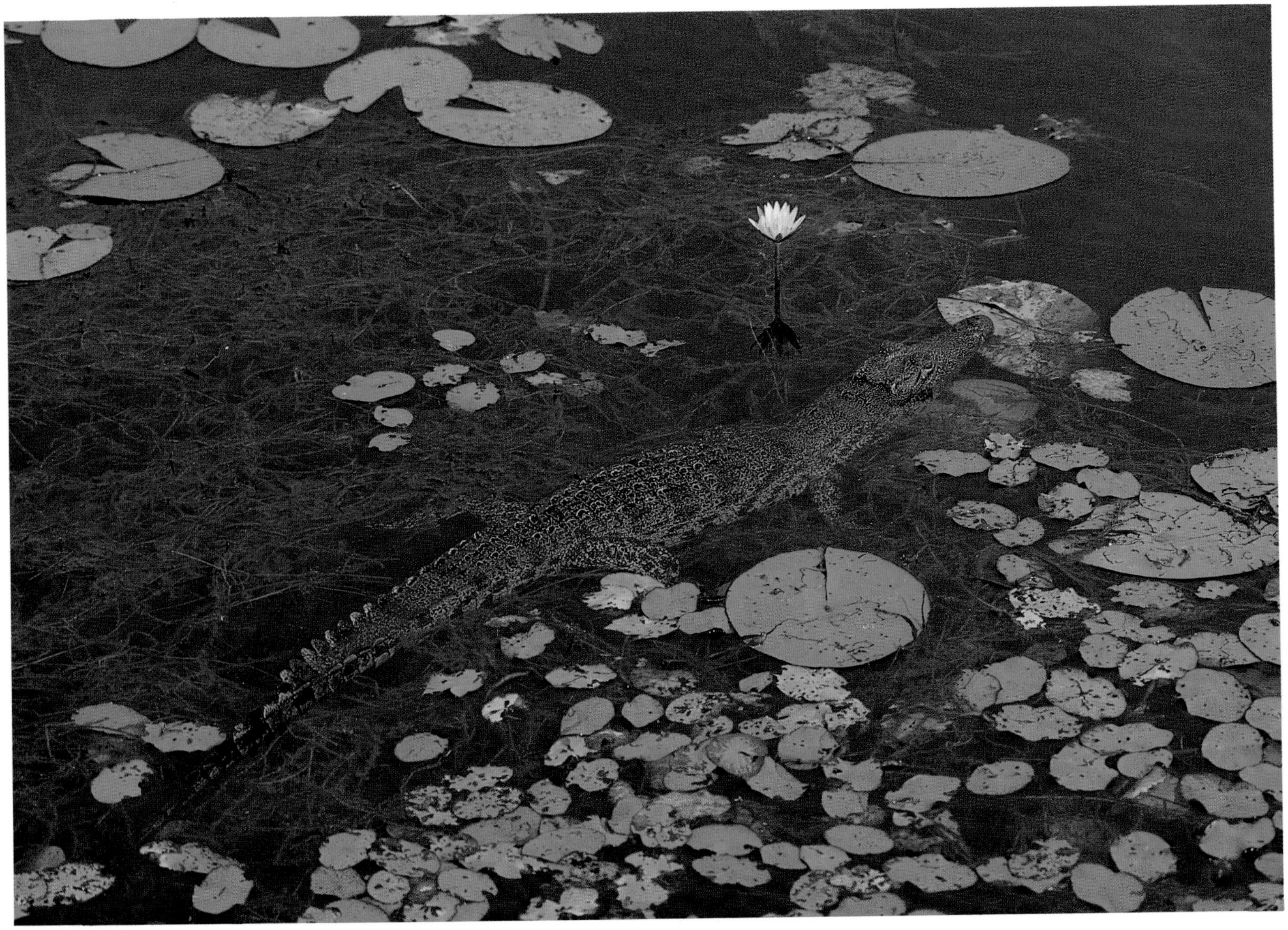

Adolescent Nile crocodiles often frequent isolated pools and backwaters, away from the dangers of conflict with their larger relatives. Especially during the mating season, threats from adults of their own species are very real for smaller animals.

OPPOSITE PAGE

Hatchling crocodiles are vulnerable to a wide variety of predators, from herons and fish eagles to terrapins and catfish. They normally remain in a group near their mother until they are too large to be taken.

Muggers lay their eggs in a hole dug in sandy soil near water. When the hatchlings emerge, they emit chirping noises which attract the parents, who then carry them to the water. Eggs which are late to hatch may be cracked by the parents to release the baby crocodiles.

The eggs of a saltwater crocodile. Each nest may contain between twenty and ninety eggs, 50–95mm (1¼–2½in) in length, weighing 50–150 grammes (2–6oz). They hatch in about ninety days, aided by the heat generated by the decaying vegetation of the nest.

METABOLISM & MOVEMENT

For a superficially primitive creature, the crocodilian has a complex and fascinating lifestyle. Many of its habits arise from the fact that they have no self-regulatory system for controlling the temperature of their blood.

As they are commonly only comfortable within quite narrow temperature bands, this means that a large part of their time is devoted to finding ways of either warming their systems, or cooling them down. This can involve basking in the sun, lying in mud, floating in cooler or warmer water, or thermoregulation by means of opening their mouths wide — all of which are seen in this section.

Although the movements of crocodilians could never be described as graceful, the various species have nevertheless developed some very efficient methods of manouevering their bulky and ungainly frames around at an extraordinary rate, both in and out of the water. Many an unwary human has been surprised by the swiftness of the mugger in the 'high walk' illustrated on page 73 — a method of locomotion which also allows it to traverse great distances in search of food and water.

OPPOSITE PAGE

A dominating factor in the life of crocodilians is the need to maintain their body temperature between certain limits. Having no internal control mechanism, they must use a combination of basking and bathing to warm up or cool down.

Head raised and jaws half open, a male Nile crocodile delivers a dominance display. He produces a deep coughing or rumbling sound which warns off other large males nearby. Smaller males will already have moved away from this stretch of river bank.

Basking on the bank of a stream, a Nile crocodile seldom strays far from the water during the day. The demands of thermoregulation make it necessary from time to time to beat a retreat into the water to cool off. The muddy slide on the bank is the crocodile's route to water.

The lining of a crocodile's mouth is well supplied with blood-vessels. Basking with the mouth open increases the rate of heat exchange with the air, either to lose excess heat or to absorb heat as the day warms up.

The larger the animal, the slower it responds to changes in the temperature of its surroundings. A large Nile crocodile may need to bask for several hours to recover from the cool of the night.

OPPOSITE PAGE

In the evening, as the sun goes down, the water cools more slowly than the air. To conserve heat, crocodiles often retreat into the water at dusk.

In the early morning, a crocodile needs to bask in the sun for several hours to raise its body temperature to a functional level. Although it appears sluggish at this time of day, this is deceptive: it is capable of sudden movement if disturbed, or if potential prey appears.

As well as opening the jaws, pressing the body to the damp ground is another way in which crocodiles lose heat during the warmest part of the day.

Open river banks and the edges of reservoirs provide basking places from which muggers can quickly reach the water to cool off. Smaller animals rarely move far from water by day, because of the risk of overheating.

The saltwater crocodile's preferred temperature range is 28°–30°C (82°–86°F) by day, and 25°–27°C (77°–81°F) at night. In New Guinea the species digs a dry-season den deep enough to reach the falling water table: there is no evidence of winter dormancy in northern Australia.

The New Guinea crocodile rarely basks in direct sunlight, preferring to lie in shady places when it is on shore. It spends most of its time in the water, where birds such as gallinules and coots form the greater part of its diet.

Basking alligators can absorb heat from the ground as well as from the sun. The flow of blood to the skin is increased during warming, to increase the uptake of heat. There is evidence that large alligators are able to maintain their body temperature several degrees above that of the water in which they are submerged, presumably by generating heat within their bodies.

The spectacled caiman prefers still, open water to fast-flowing streams in shady places. Although it is mainly a freshwater species, it occurs in Trinidad and Tobago, showing considerable tolerance of salt water. Males reach about 2.5m (8ft 2in) in length; females are smaller.

OPPOSITE PAGE

Between late October and the end of March, Chinese alligators spend most of the time in burrows which they dig in banks near water. The burrow may extend 3m (10ft) or more below ground, with several openings and chambers.

A Nile crocodile leaving water often propels itself toboggan-style, using its hind legs to skid the weighty body up the bank.

A mugger moving in a 'high walk'. They are more mobile on land than most other crocodiles, able to walk long distances in search of water during the dry season.

Cruising in the water with its head raised, a male mugger establishes its territory each December, ready for the breeding season which starts in January. Slapping the water with the head is a signal to other males to keep away; it also serves to attract passing females.

HUNTING & PREY

Very few animals are safe from a full-grown crocodilian if they are foolish enough to come within striking distance: the Nile crocodile commonly takes zebra and wildebeeste; the saltwater crocodile preys on buffalo and kangeroo; and the American alligator hunts raccoons and young cattle. All of these species will also take men, and few years pass without a number of human fatalities.

The principal hunting tactic is to approach by stealth, submerged underwater, to within a few feet of their unwary prey, and then to spring out, often several yards up the bank, with amazing agility. Once the prey is held it is not normally savaged to death, but rather dragged back in the water and drowned. For smaller prey, the usual method of despatch is a lightening quick sideways swipe of the snout.

OPPOSITE PAGE

Chinese alligators include frogs in their diet, though they more usually hunt in water.

BELOW

A Nile crocodile drowning an impala buck. In muddy rivers and waterholes, the crocodile sees animals drinking, selects the place where it will attack, and then approaches from a distance submerged underwater. Its stealthy movement produces no ripples to warn its victim, until the final lunge.

ABOVE

Warthogs are frequently caught at waterholes by lurking crocodiles. The initial attack often kills the warthog by breaking its neck; if it survives the first impact it will drown when the crocodile drags it into deeper water.

Crocodiles catch their prey with a sudden sideways sweep of the jaws. Even on land, birds are not immune from capture by an alert crocodile.

Large muggers often take small prey. Here a shoal of fish fry is under attack. The bonus to the mugger comes when larger fish also attack the shoal, and fall prey to the crocodile. Insects found in crocodile stomaches may often have been caught by another animal, such as a frog, which the mugger has eaten.

OPPOSITE PAGE
A marsh mugger taking a python. Fully-grown, these Indian crocodiles are capable of killing hoofed mammals as big as sambar or gaur (the Indian bison). Their more normal diet is catfish, small mammals, and occasionally birds.

The mugger includes carrion in its diet, here a gaur drowned in the river.

The mugger's diet is often said to include human remains floating downstream from the ghats *(riverside steps from which the dead are launched on their final journey) where they have been partially cremated. There is no evidence that this occasional taste of human flesh gives rise to man-eating.*

Johnston's crocodile grows to only 2.5m (8ft) in length. Its prey consists mostly of amphibians, reptiles, and fish, with occasional birds and small mammals. It lies in wait for passing prey, grabbing it with swift sideways movements of its head.

OPPOSITE PAGE

Muggers have been known to eat birds, but the chances of catching a river cormorant by chasing a flock are somewhat slender. Nevertheless, the mugger's speed across the ground for short distances gives it a good chance of catching the occasional wounded or sick bird.

The spectacled caiman lives in a range extending from southern Mexico to subtropical South America around the border between Paraguay and Argentina. It feeds on prey ranging in size from snails and frogs to large catfish and small deer.

OPPOSITE PAGE

Chinese alligators often spend the day lying up in burrows dug for hibernation during the dry winter. They emerge in the evening in search of prey such as turtles and crustaceans; in cultivated areas they will also take chickens and small dogs at night.

The false gavial can grow to 5.5m (18ft) in length. It lives in the swamps and freshwater rivers of Borneo, Sumatra, and the Malay peninsula. Its jaw structure suggests that it lives mainly on fish, but hunters use live monkeys (crab-eating macaques) as bait to catch false gavials, and there is at least one account of such a monkey being taken from a river bank in the wild.

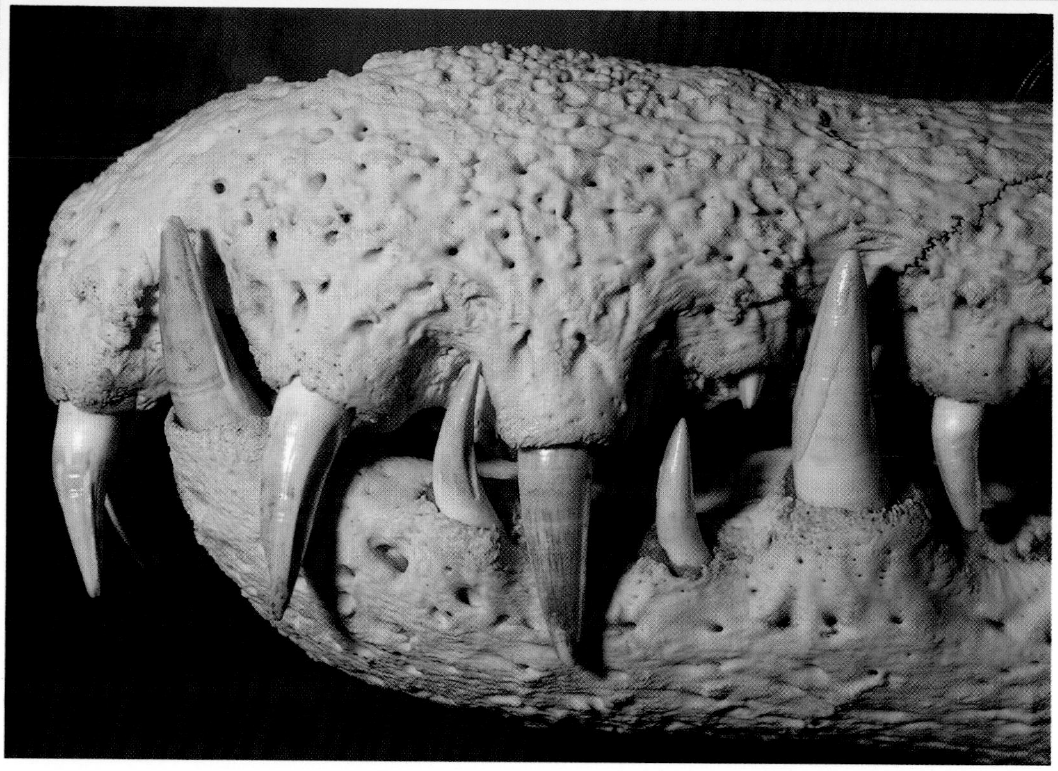

ABOVE

A gavial has about 100 teeth, those of the upper and lower jaws interlocking to improve its grip on fish. Its slender jaws are not very strong, but can be moved quickly and accurately in the water.

RIGHT

The teeth of a gavial interlock to improve its grip on its prey, mostly fish. In this dry skull, the outward projection of the teeth is clearly visible, together with their narrow, claw-like shape.

LOCATION & HABITAT

Though now hunted out of vast reaches of their earlier terrain, species of crocodilian are still found, albeit in smaller numbers and more tightly-knit communities, in most areas of the world — from China, South-East Asia, the Indian subcontinent and South America; to North America, Australasia, and Africa. Their range is limited to the tropical and subtropical regions of these countries and continents, as crocodilians, with the exception of the slightly hardier American alligator, do not dwell in locations where the temperature regularly falls below 10°C–15°C (50°–59°F).

The habitats adopted by individual species are many and various, ranging from the banks of the slow-moving Ganges beneath the beautiful peaks of the Himalayas, to the hauntingly still swamps of the Florida Everglades, and the crashing breakers and deserted beaches of the North Australian coastline — all of which and many more are illustrated in this section.

OPPOSITE PAGE
The Orinoco crocodile is a freshwater species. It wanders overland during the rainy season to find quiet pools, away from the swift-flowing rivers. Individuals found in Trinidad probably arrived by 'passive migration' – that is, they drifted from the mouth of the Orinoco River on rafts of vegetation.

During the cold season, Nile crocodiles lie up in burrows dug in the bank of a watercourse. Often each burrow has several inhabitants, who have co-operated in the digging, carrying mouthfuls of earth down to the water, where they wash it out of their jaws by shaking their heads underwater. Sometimes, however, the largest individual subsequently evicts the rest, becoming the sole occupant. Here one such dominant male emerges into the warmer weather, alone, from a burrow which may have been dug by a group working together.

Saltwater crocodiles have an enormous distribution range, from Cochin on the west coast of India, via Bangladesh, the Philippines, Indonesia, New Guinea and northern Australia to Fiji. They are capable of inhabiting salt water indefinitely, and of travelling great distances by sea.

Johnston's crocodile is usually referred to as a 'freshwater crocodile', though it can tolerate a relatively high degree of salinity. It is restricted to inland locations in northern Australia because the habitat nearer the sea is occupied by saltwater crocodiles. Where the larger saltwater species has been hunted out, Johnston's crocodile is able to live in brackish water.

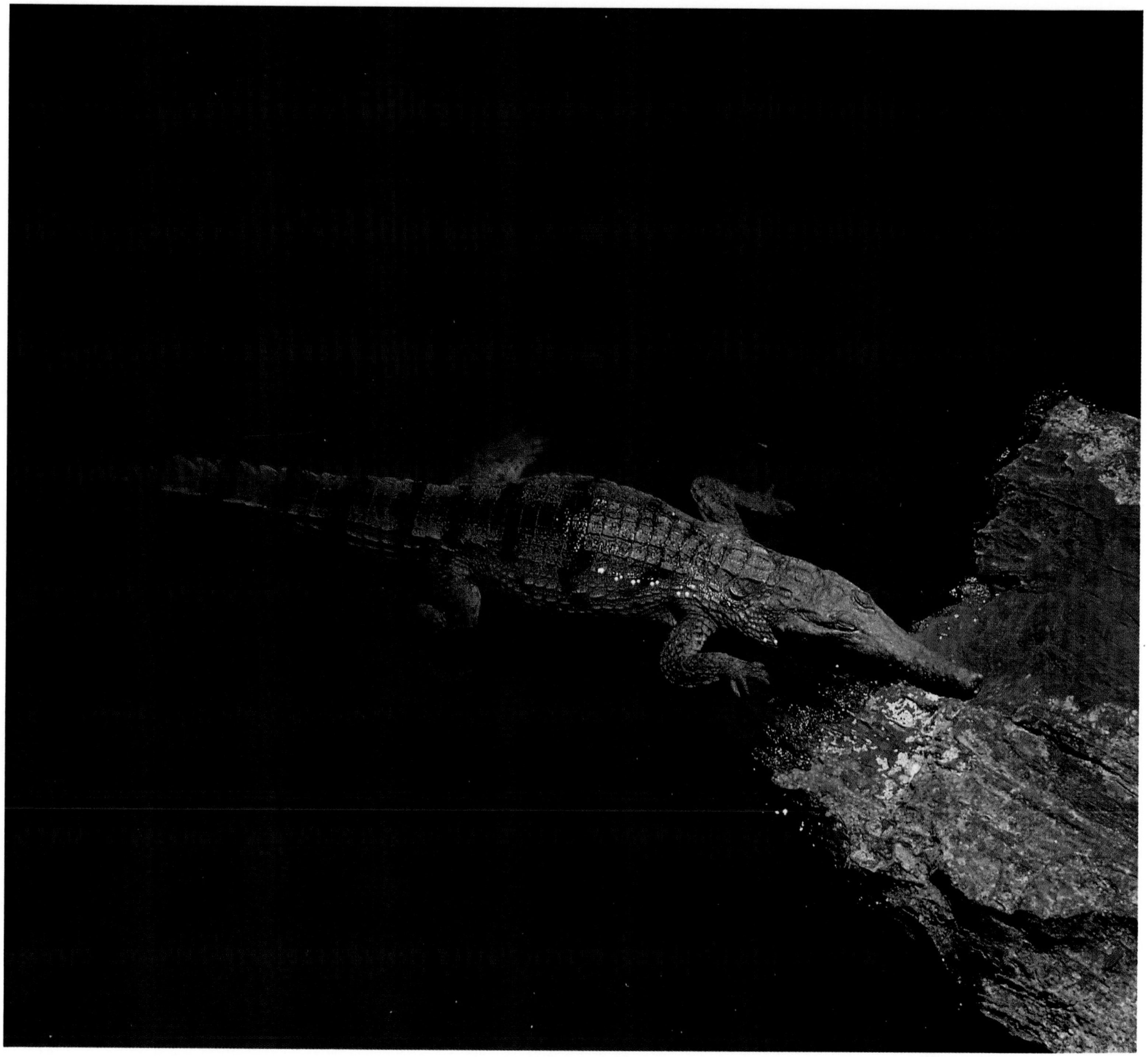

Johnston's crocodile in Belli Glen Gorge, Northern Territory. During the dry season, individuals may travel considerable distances overland in search of isolated pools. They have been known to return to a pool used the previous year from as far as 40km (25 miles) away.

Siamese crocodiles grow to about 3.5m (11ft 5in) long. They live along rainforest rivers, and in nearby swamps and lagoons. Their diet consists mainly of fish.

Morelet's crocodile lives in eastern Mexico, Belize, and northern Guatemala. A freshwater species, it avoids large rivers, living instead in savannah ponds, lakes, and marshy areas in the rainforest. It grows to about 3m (10ft) long.

The American crocodile tolerates a narrow temperature range: in water cooler than about 18°C (65°F) it becomes torpid and drowns. It can live in salt water as well as fresh, growing to about 5m (16ft 5 in) long. It is now very rare throughout its range because of over-hunting.

Small (less than 2m (7ft) in length) and heavily armoured, the West African Dwarf crocodile is considered to be a primitive species. It lives mainly in swamps and sluggish streams in the rainforest areas of west and central Africa.

'Gator holes as much as 8m (26ft) across dug by alligators retain water in the dry season. The alligator uses its hole as a place to keep cool during the heat of the day. Disused (they hope) 'gator holes are a valuable refuge during dry weather for a wide variety of other animals.

OPPOSITE PAGE

In the dwarf cypress swamps of Florida's Everglades, an American alligator works at excavating a 'gator hole. Females dig holes near their nests, releasing the babies into them when they hatch so that they can be more easily defended against predation.

The stronghold of the gavial is in the tributaries of the Ganges, including those which flow through the terai *(belts of marshy, jungly land) of southern Nepal. It has become very scarce as a result of human persecution, though as a predator on catfish, which themselves do serious damage to the important tilapia fisheries, the gavial is a beneficial species to man.*

With the Himalayas in the background, a gavial basks on a sandbank in Royal Chitwan National Park. The species is endangered mainly because its eggs are collected as food; it also drowns in fishing nets. In Pakistan it is hunted for its skin.

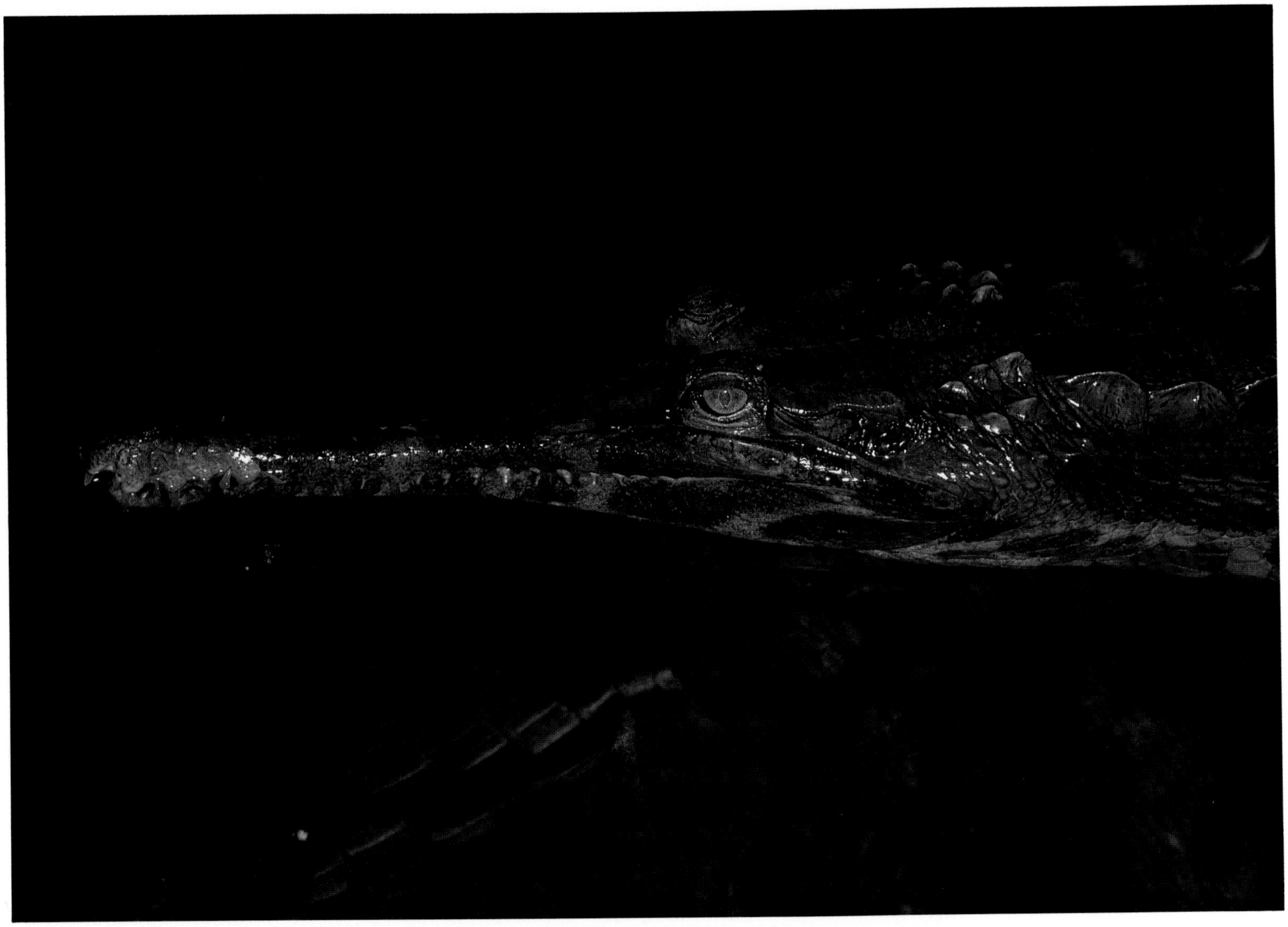

Gavials live mainly in deep, fast-flowing rivers. They are not strong swimmers, being poorly streamlined, but their slender jaws are ideally adapted for their method of feeding, making sudden sideway lunges as prey comes into range.

OPPOSITE PAGE

Saltwater crocodiles may travel far inland, displacing Johnston's crocodiles from freshwater streams and billabongs. Until the salty's numbers declined, the freshwater species was unable to expand its range.

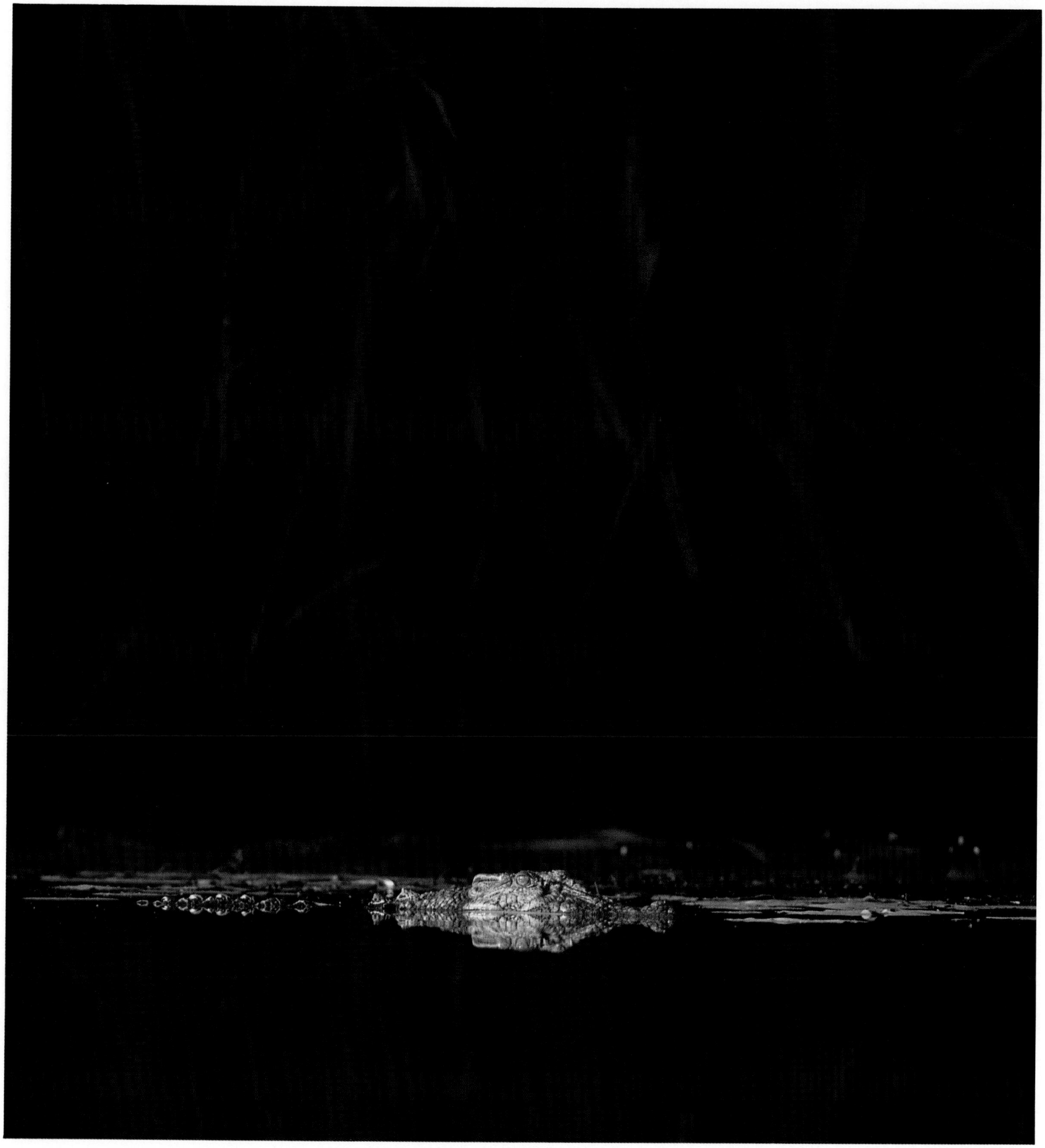

CROCODILIANS & MAN

Though man views the crocodilian with fear, the damage it has done to humankind is miniscule compared to the devastation that humans have wrought on the crocodilians of the world. Motivated by fear, vengeance, greed, and, regrettably, simple spite, man has wiped out whole crocodilian populations, or driven them from the support of their established habitats to gradually diminish in numbers and body size in unsuitable environments (most species are not nearly as large now as the biggest known examples of their type recorded even in very recent history).

Fortunately there has been a change in attitude in the past few years, with legislation in many areas which is intended, if properly enforced, to offer protection to crocodilians — the majority of species now being officially listed as endangered. Allied to the increase in commercial farming — which is examined here — which can, if sympathetically operated, offer many conservational benefits, and the general modern distaste for and decline in the wearing and use of animal skins, there may yet be hope for the future.

OPPOSITE PAGE
The Chinese alligator is an endangered species, surviving only in a restricted area away from the densest human settlement.

ABOVE

The unacceptable face of crocodilism. A full-grown Nile crocodile has not an enemy in the world, nor, in natural conditions, any great need of friends. Conservation of crocodilians in the face of over-hunting is made more difficult by the public image of crocodiles as cruel man-eating predators.

LEFT

A young Nile crocodile is a better advertisement for its species. Its bright eye, small teeth, and attractive coloration make it more acceptable to the public than the fearsome monster it will become if it survives to adulthood.

The Nile crocodile was extinct in the Nile delta by 1700, and rare below Aswan by 1900. It is under threat from hunting everywhere in Africa except in a few well-managed National Parks.

OPPOSITE PAGE

The Orinoco crocodile has a reputation for attacking its human neighbours. However, the reduced size of contemporary specimens makes this unlikely today. Specimens shot in 1800 measured between 5–6m (16ft 5in–20ft) long; in the twentieth century none has exceeded 4m (13ft 2in).

ABOVE

In the 1920s, Morelet's crocodile was very common around Belize City. Since then, hunting and the destruction of its habitat have reduced its population until it is now quite rare.

RIGHT

A large adult mugger basking in the sun. They seldom exceed five metres in length. Most are much smaller because of the pressure of hunting: larger individuals are the favoured prey of poachers because they provide broader skins.

The American alligator is large and powerful enough to drag a full-grown man into the water. During the settlement of the southern United States, alligators were hunted throughout their range, and became very wary of man. In those states where legislation was passed to protect them after the Second World War, alligators lost their fear, and once more became aggressive towards humans.

The gavial is regarded as harmless to man, although it grows to over 6m (20ft) long. Its long, slender jaws represent the extreme development of the fish-eating crocodilian, sacrificing strength for manoeuvrability in the water.

When European settlers first arrived in North America, alligators were very common, spreading from what was to become eastern Texas to the southeastern tip of Virginia. Their principal haunts were the swamps extending along large parts of the eastern seaboard, which became places of terror to the settlers.

Alligators kept in captivity become increasingly hostile to humans, presumably because they learn that people are no longer to be feared. In the wild, over most of their range, alligators are usually timid and retiring, because of fear induced by their history of persecution.

The Chinese alligator is the closest relative of the American alligator. It is only half the size, modern specimens not exceeding 1.5m (5ft) in length. Records show that in historical times individuals reached 3m (10ft): persecution by hunting, mostly in defence of newly-drained farmland, has reduced the life-expectancy of almost all crocodilians.

OPPOSITE PAGE

The Chinese alligator is most commonly found today in grassy country surrounding hill-country pools, at about 100m (328ft) above sea-level, having been driven from the coastal plains by agriculture. The surviving alligators on the plains are threatened by land drainage and the use of toxic agricultural chemicals.

Wholesale exploitation of crocodilian populations for their skins has caused a severe decline in almost every species. The softer skin of belly and flanks is the most saleable product, being used for shoes, belts, handbags, suitcases, and watch-straps. Most recently, 'personal organizers' expensively bound in crocodile or alligator skin have been fashionable among the thoughtless rich. Crocodilian populations expand very slowly: they are unable to recover from the level of hunting which is encouraged by the lucrative trade in skins.

The skin of a saltwater crocodile.

Baby New Guinea crocodiles hatched from wild-collected eggs.

OPPOSITE PAGE
Hatchling Johnston's crocodiles at a crocodile farm in Darwin, Australia.

New Guinea crocodiles growing on a farm at Port Moresby, Papua New Guinea.

OPPOSITE PAGE

American alligator farms are licensed on condition that they return a proportion of their product to the wild.

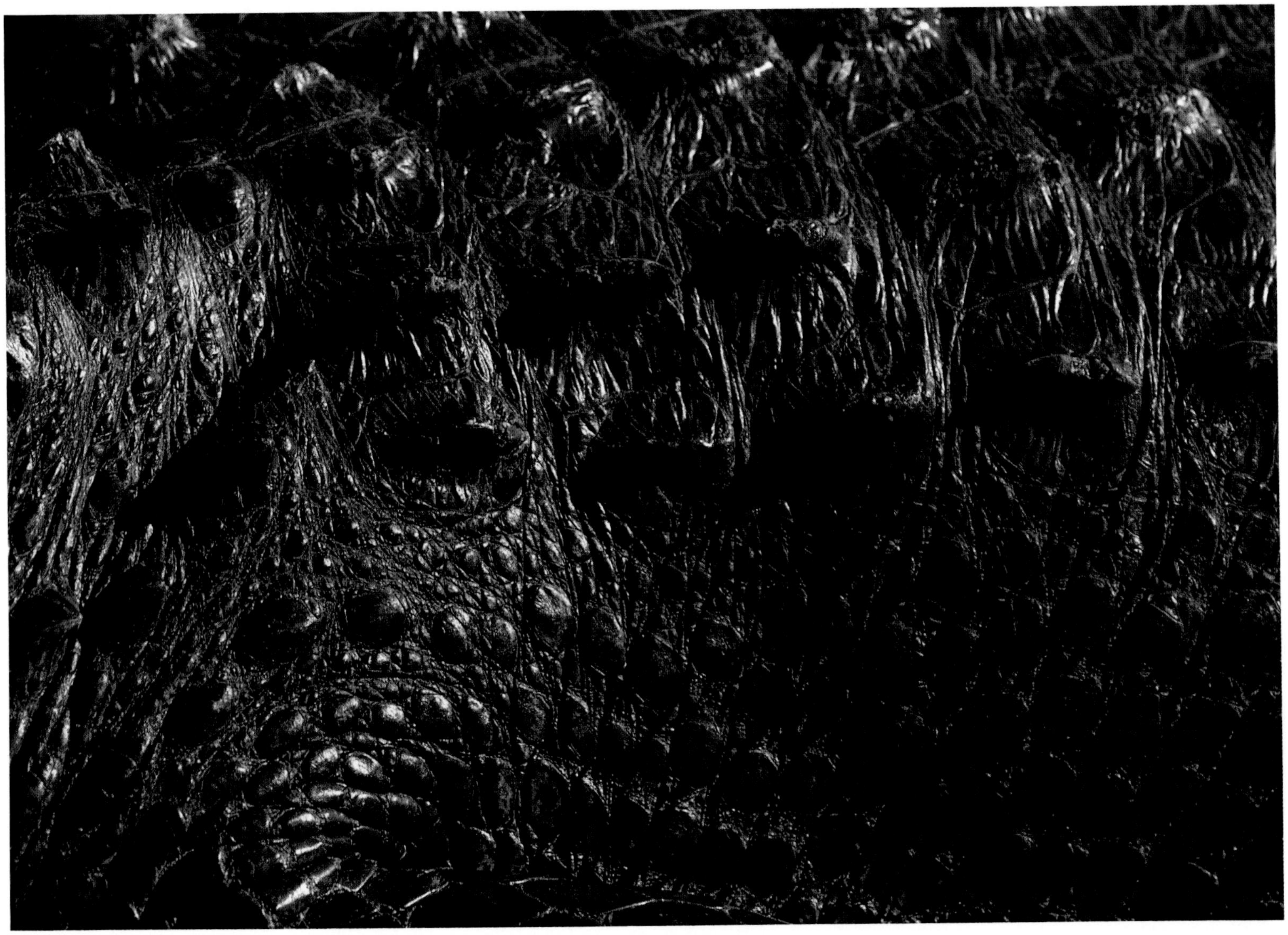

The skin of an American alligator.

In the wild, only 2 or 3 per cent of crocodilian eggs produce hatchlings which eventually grow to be adult. Farming crocodiles is one way of reducing these losses, by protecting the eggs from the dangers of predation, cannibalism, and the vagaries of the weather. Of the two types of crocodilian farm, those based on captive-laid eggs make the better contribution to conservation. State-licensed farms which concentrate on rearing eggs collected from wild nests are supposed in most countries to return a proportion of the hatchlings to the wild. Unfortunately, the financial rewards involved often make this option unattractive to the farmers.

OPPOSITE PAGE
The Siamese crocodile is hunted for food as well as skins; it is now virtually extinct in the wild, though it breeds successfully in captivity, in crocodile farms.

INDEX